FUNDAMENTAL LIFE SKILLS FOR TEENS

9 EPIC WAYS TO PREPARE FOR ADULTHOOD, BUILD SELF-CONFIDENCE, ACHIEVE PERSONAL GROWTH, MANAGE MONEY, AND ATTAIN REAL SUCCESS

JOURNEY WELLS

CONTENTS

INTRODUCTION

"Being a teenager is an amazing time and a hard time. It's when you make your best friends... You get the best and the worst as a teen. You have the best friendships and the worst heartbreaks."

— SOPHIA BUSH

I'm sure you recognize this line:

"Why can't you be more like Leo? He's good at everything."

As a teenager, this was the worst thing I had to hear from my parents. No matter how much I achieved, all I got was a list of names of almost everyone they knew who were better than me. At first, I decided to patiently digest the words but, one day, I had enough. I took matters into my own hands and decided to exceed my classmates and cousins who were, according to my parents, so much better than me, at everything. Surprisingly, I found out that they, too, were being compared to others and were being told the same things, almost word for word, by their parents.

So, why do parents do that in the first place?

I wondered if there were some secret benefits to comparing your child with others. Knowing myself, I would have spent my life searching for those secrets, but I chose to detach myself from the bitterness that was ruining my teenage years so that I could enjoy them to the best I could. And I did!

You might be wondering how I managed that seemingly incredible feat. I learned from it. I achieved it by constantly working on my thoughts and feelings. Whenever I encounter difficult tasks, I muster up the courage and put all my effort into doing them. I tried several things, but the most effective ones were none other than a handful of skills that changed my life. I call them the nine epic ways to prepare for adulthood.

But first, let me ask you this question…

What does a successful life mean to you?

If you have always wanted to be an expert in areas like time management, social interaction, and financial literacy, know that you are not alone. Millions of teens across the US are struggling with the exact same things. A few eye-opening statistics are testimony to this fact. For instance, around 83% of teens do not know how to manage money, and 87% do not know about personal finance. Despite this fact, 35% of teens want to learn how to save, and 28% know how important managing a budget is. They don't have the required skills to put these wishes into action.

Anxiety levels are rising. The National Institutes of Health reports that one in three teens aged thirteen to eighteen will experience an anxiety disorder. Numbers have risen steadily over the years due to high expectations and the pressure to succeed, threatening environments, and the effects of social media.

About 96% of parents in the US feel it is important for their children to know how to cook or bake. However, only 33% cook with their children weekly, and 64% of people do not have a high level of confidence in their children's ability to follow a recipe.

Around 25% of parents feel that they are the main barrier to their teen becoming more independent. Many parents or guardians take charge of nearly all home tasks because it is easier to do so than to teach their teens these skills.

Do you know how to cook a proper, nutritious meal for yourself?

Parents of every age have made the common mistake of burdening their children with unrealistic expectations. While their sentiments might be to make their child a better human, a better person, they often fail to understand that the ways they choose to make their children better can have a negative impact on their children's psychological health.

But just because your parents have made some mistakes doesn't mean you can use them as an excuse to let yourself fail in life. You have the strength to become the best version of yourself. And to do so, you need to learn some essential skills. The good news about life skills is that nobody is born with them; each skill, ability, and talent can be learned. Therefore, if you aren't great at baking, find it hard to start a conversation with new people, or tend to let stress get the better of you, it could be that you haven't honed these skills yet.

There isn't a magic lamp you rub when you become an adult that gives you automatic access to all these skills. Instead, these skills need to be learned, preferably as early as possible so that you can become a natural at them. In learning, you will make mistakes. These mistakes will help you avoid even bigger ones later in life that can affect your financial and personal future. As our favorite character, *Hopper,* in the TV show *Stranger Things* says:

"Make mistakes, learn from them, and when life hurts you, because it will, remember the hurt. The hurt is good. It means you're out of that cave."

Not knowing how to cook or saving money through budgeting might not be "the end of the world" that your parents keep insisting on, but failing to hone life skills before you become a college student or leave the family home can have significant and altering consequences. For instance, most college students do not know how to invest, manage their student loans, or plan financially for their future. This can interfere with a myriad of goals they have when they graduate, including buying a home and a vehicle.

Do you fear that you might not be prepared for life after you leave your home?

Success is not exclusively centered on financial stability, of course. Think of happiness as having numerous filled "bottles" —the bottle of friendship, academic success, health and fitness, contentment with one's home life, and more.

Working as a teacher for many years, I've come across several issues that teens face. My extensive experience has taught me how teens are affected by different life situations. However, they hold the strength to modify their problems and find solutions. The knowledge I am sharing with you has taken my entire profession to compile. I am ready to help you feel better about yourself, free up time, and "fill all your bottles," as I do with all my students.

Many influencers and celebrities you follow are struggling (or have done so) with similar problems. For instance, Olivia Rodrigo says she never felt attractive when growing up because she was not "traditionally pretty." To curb her stress, she decided to spend less time online, saying, "You can create your own reality sometimes with social media. What you see just becomes your reality, and it's totally not at all."

Success and happiness are difficult if you neglect key life skills. Therefore, I have included the essential skills you need to be more confident, healthy, sociable, financially savvy, and all-around happy. With all the easily learned and life-changing skills mentioned in this book, I will be providing you with practical strategies that you can start applying in your daily life immediately. Once you gain the knowledge and skills, achieving your goals will become easy.

You must remember that no one can induce a positive change in your life. It's only you who can work hard and achieve your dreams. Changes are hard to make. During your journey, you will face a massive number of hurdles. Remaining steadfast and consistent in working for your goal will make you succeed. There's a whole world for you to discover.

Not only will you learn new things, but it will also help you recognize the mistakes you might have made and how you can avoid them. This time of your life is, undoubtedly, the most precious one. Ensuring you live it to the fullest by enjoying and learning as much as possible will build a robust and positive foundation for the rest of your life. You can achieve goals you may never have imagined possible through commitment, discipline, and a wish to be more well-rounded.

Now, you may ask what makes me the right person to guide you? Well, it's because what is written in this book has been tried and tested. I have combined all my personal and professional experiences, along with prominent research in the field of teenage life skills, so that you get all the information in one place rather than opening 100 tabs at once on your P.C.

In this book, I will share the nine essential skills you need to master to be a successful, confident, and happy teen who is ready to take on the world and beyond. I will share the latest information on how to be the best at these skills, and by the time you finish reading this book, you will know how to:

- Make friends and communicate well with others.
- Remain strong and resilient when challenging times come.
- Excel at problem-solving and use time wisely.
- Give due importance to your physical and mental health.
- Make home chores easy and become a savvy cook.
- Be ready for college and your first job.
- Save money and start making your first investments.
- Stay safe online and when you're out and about.
- Make a first impression by dressing like a boss.

It's time to stop looking down on yourself and boost your self-esteem. I want you to sit in the driver's seat of your own life, and when you do, I promise you that you can achieve any dream or goal you set your mind to. Let's continue reading so that you discover yourself, and we can work together on polishing your abilities for a successful, independent, and happy future!

1

SKILL ONE: PERFECTING YOUR SOCIAL SKILLS AND COMMUNICATING EFFECTIVELY WITH OTHERS

"The most important thing in communication is hearing what isn't said."

— PETER DRUCKER

LEARNING TO COMMUNICATE WITH OTHERS

Communicating with others can be difficult during your teen years because teens undergo a myriad of hormonal changes, and the brain is constantly developing. Therefore, you may find it harder to control your impulses and read others' emotions. For instance, research published in the Journal of Nonverbal Behavior states that teens, aged thirteen to fifteen, can find it harder to determine what someone is saying based on their tone of voice. It is particularly true for emotions like anger, joy, disgust, or happiness.

During this age, an urgency prevails in every action taken (Why Teenagers Are So Impulsive, 2023). For instance, you want to become popular on social media or become the best at a sport. And technically, there is nothing wrong with getting things done fast. Starting early in any field of life is one of the golden rules to success. But do you know why? It is because once you start doing something, it's very likely that you will make mistakes. Starting early will give you time and space to learn from your mistakes and improve your weak points.

On the other hand, there are drawbacks to impulsive behavior (Leuker & Van Den Bos, 2016). Deciding instantly and diving into things without proper understanding and knowledge is not a wise thing to do. You can make poor decisions and get stuck in a tricky situation or make a commitment you can't fulfill.

Another challenge you may face is thinking that you know what's best. Not that you're wrong. Being constantly in sync with the changing world, teenagers have a particular advantage regarding knowledge of technology and happenings around the world. But there's a lack of experience, which can often lead to making regrettable decisions. In other words, you lack the critical knowledge that can only be gained through experiences. So, stubbornness and rigidity in behaviors can cause you some serious problems.

Now, what is it that you find yourself struggling with as a teenager?

Do you struggle to control your emotions, or do you act impulsively? Make a list of all such character traits that you have. Keep it with you while you read this chapter, as you will be provided with tips to overcome all the challenges you have been facing. The following communication strategies are what you might have been searching for.

So, without further ado, let's dive straight into them.

1: Knowing and Regulating Your Emotions

Emotions are directly connected to the psychological state of an individual. Your permanent emotional state is governed by several factors, including your past experiences, bonding with friends and family, your upbringing, and a lot more.

However, your momentary emotional state will fluctuate. Because your brain is developing, and you are constantly growing and learning from your environment. All of this makes you vulnerable to being affected by things happening around you. So, if you like something, it will make you happy instantly. Whereas if you don't approve of something, it will provoke immediate, and oftentimes explosive anger in you. In other words, things around you are a stimulus and give rise to your emotions. Most often, you end up expressing it.

Expressing emotions openly has its pros and cons. If we talk about expressing happiness, that can be beneficial. On the other hand, the expression of anger can give birth to several problems.

By no means am I suggesting concealing your emotions. That is a completely different thing and can be very unhealthy in many cases. It is all about filtering your emotions before expressing them, as there is more than one way to vocalize a single statement.

Let's say you are mad at your friend for not letting you know about a class test, and as a result, you scored badly. In that case, instead of shouting at them and cutting them out of your life, you can simply express your disappointment through words.

"Listen, I am sure you didn't intend to do it, but I am a little upset and need some time to be by myself. I hope you understand. I will soon catch up."

In your teen years, you can find it harder to control your impulses and emotions. Therefore, it is important to know how to identify your emotions and respond appropriately to tense situations.

Now, how can you control your emotions and express them in a better way?

First, you must be aware of your momentary emotional state. At any given time, you should be aware of the emotions you are experiencing. The easiest way of doing this is by using Dr. Plutchik's Wheel.

Fun Fact: Did you know that there are 42 facial muscles that people use to express their emotions? Amazing right? This means that when you smile, you are using those 42 muscles. Similarly, for showing disgust, anger, or hatred, you are using 42 facial muscles (*Dean, 2022*).

Plutchik's wheel and the eight primary emotions

According to the Psychologist and University Professor, Dr. Robert Plutchik, there are eight primary emotions, namely:

- Anger
- Fear
- Sadness
- Disgust
- Surprise
- Anticipation
- Trust
- Joy

In Dr. Plutchik's wheel, he arranged these eight emotions with colors to show that emotions can range from intense to mild. For example, fear, in its most intense form, can be terror, while in its mildest form, it is mere apprehension (Seconds, 2022). Similarly, trust in its most intense form can be admiration, while in its mildest form, it is acceptance. The most intense form of anger can be rage and its mildest form is annoyance and so on.

With the help of Dr. Plutchik's wheel, you can pinpoint the exact emotion you are feeling. This will help you become aware of your psychological state. Once you have identified your emotion, take a moment, and think about some possible ways in which you can express it. Quickly visualize the consequences your reaction can have.

Another thing you can do is think of how your ideal personality would have behaved if they were standing in your shoes. By processing all of it in your brain, before expressing your emotion, you will get an idea of what needs to be done and can significantly lower the chances of negative consequences (Karimova, 2023).

Activity

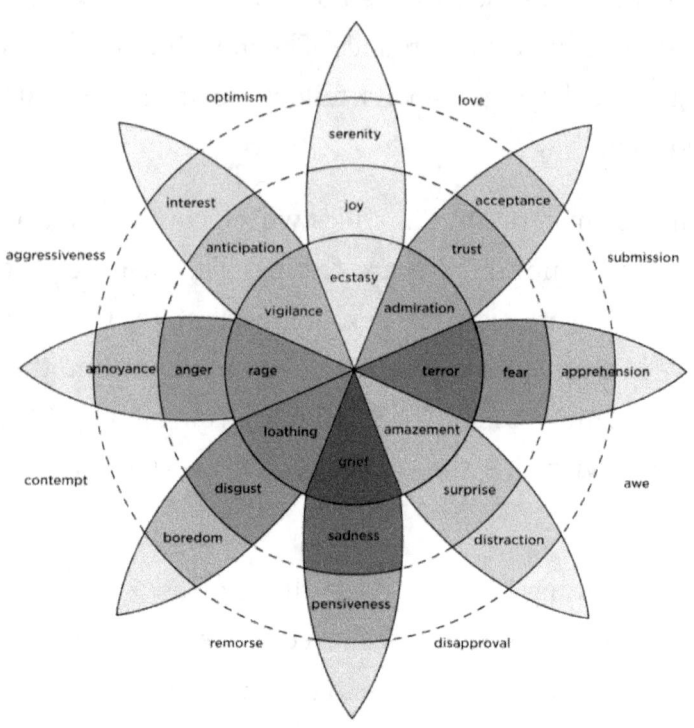

Print a copy of Dr. Plutchik's Wheel and keep it easily accessible. When you experience any kind of stimuli, pull out the wheel and try to identify the emotion you are feeling. Keep a journal and write down the different emotions you feel throughout the day. Write down how you dealt with this emotion. After a day has passed, go back to your journal, and ask yourself if you could have dealt with this emotion in a better way, or if you are happy with how you expressed it.

2: Calming Down

Oftentimes, teenagers tend to act impulsively. This might not affect you at the time but developing a habit of impulsivity can prove devastating. Many still insist on acting on impulse because they haven't been told that all it takes is a pause.

Whenever a tense situation arises, all you need to do is step back and pause. Tell yourself that you won't simply "react" impulsively to the incident. Instead, try to express yourself calmly with the person you are interacting with, using an open mind and expressing yourself in a relaxed, rational way. You should understand that in an argument, both sides believe they are right. The only way to put an end to the argument is if both sides try to understand each other's points of view.

Think of a person who raises their voice during an argument. Now imagine someone who's calm and composed. Who do you think will win the argument and get their point across? If you pick the calm and composed one, then you are right! This is because they listen to opponents and express their opinions in a rational organized way. The charisma in the personality of a person who remains calm is unmatched. Remember that raising your voice won't earn you the attention and respect you desire from others. The act of maintaining composure in the face of challenges is what will attract people to you.

Now imagine yourself sitting in a job interview and the interviewer tells you they don't find you suitable for the job. What reaction can leave a good impression? Letting your anger or denial show on your face, or smiling politely and saying a nice goodbye? The latter depicts more maturity, acceptance of one's flaws, and willingness to work on them. So always remember that by expressing yourself calmly, you are more likely to be truly heard.

3: Resolving Conflicts Successfully and Being an Active Listener

Encountering conflict as a teenager is very common and consequently hard to handle. The tricky part about conflicts is that it's not about convincing others that you are right, and they are wrong, but it is about being open to others' perspectives. That is because both sides think they are in the right, and neither of the two groups in a conflict is willing to understand and let go of their opinions long enough to realize that both sides can be right or entirely wrong.

In your teenage years, it is easy to get into arguments with friends and even family members. In the same way you want to be heard, others want you to listen to them. In winning an argument, you would never want to lose a good friend. Would you? Whenever a conflict arises, try to imagine that you and the other person/s are on the same soccer team, and your aim is to score a goal. Successful conflict resolution involves being a team player and valuing the needs and desires of others as much as you value your own.

To solve a conflict with others, follow these steps:

a: Try to define the Problem

If you are working on a team project at school and both of you want to take care of the graphic design aspect, you might say, "Okay, so the issue we are having is that both of us want to do the graphic design part and nobody wants to do the text." Identifying the issue emphasizes the problem to be solved and somewhat depersonalizes it.

Sometimes the cause of an issue is completely illogical, but because nobody focuses on it and everyone keeps insisting upon their opinion, the issue remains unresolved.

b: Listen to the points of view of the other person or people

Practice active listening skills so the people you are interacting with feel truly heard. Avoid interrupting them, not really listening to them, or hoping they finish talking quickly so you can jump in and give your point of view (Staff, 2022). The elements of active listening are:

- Using open body language. Leave your arms at the sides of your body instead of crossing your arms over your chest. Face the person speaking, look them in the eye, and aim to maintain a friendly expression. Nod your head occasionally to show you are listening.
- Using phrases that show you understand them. Useful phrases include, "I understand," "I get you," and "You have a good point."
- Being patient while others are speaking and giving your point of view when they are done speaking. Make sure your tone of voice is calm and avoid speaking at a loud volume or speaking too quickly (as this may indicate you are tense).
- Clarifying doubts by asking questions. This will enable you to work out their concerns and wishes. Sometimes, you might think someone is

upset because of one thing, but their concern is not what you imagine.

c: Understand that people have different conflict styles

During a conflict, you must respect that not everyone has the same style. If you have a friend who likes taking a break when an argument arises, acknowledge their need for space and get back to the discussion when things have calmed down. Some people need a little distance when things get tense, while others seek communication and prefer to resolve problems immediately. If you are familiar with the person's conflict style, try accommodating their need. After all, not being on the same page over an issue should not affect your relationship with the person. Do it if they need you to support them and be by their side. Otherwise, give them the space, and things will get better.

Use your journal to write down your conflict style. Do you think conflict styles can vary from person to person? For Example, you might need some space after an argument with your friend. Whereas, after an argument with your siblings, you might find yourself seeking their company.

d: Employ effective Language

The use of words is a real game changer when it comes to resolving a conflict. Your opponents don't want to be defeated. They want to win, so they probably won't even listen to the valid arguments you present. However, by using the right words, you can make them feel that both of you are on the same team. You are not against them. You are just giving them a suggestion that can be beneficial.

When you are talking to others, avoid behaviors such as blaming, judging, or criticizing, as these can make them become defensive. Avoid "you" phrases, such as "You always" and "You never", and focus on "I" phrases instead. For instance, you might say, "When you have a sleepover and don't invite me, I feel left out." That sounds much better than saying, "You always have sleepovers, and you never invite me."

4: Expressing Empathy

We are usually unaware of the difficulties people around us might be experiencing. It can sometimes be hard to express empathy when you are a teen, and there is a scientific reason for that: the area of the brain involved in empathy (the medial prefrontal cortex) is underused in teenagers. According to the study, as an individual grows from teenager to adult, their brain activity shifts from the back of the mind to the front. So, a teenager might judge a person, whereas an adult will feel empathetic toward the same person (Teenage Brain Lacks Empathy, 2006).

The good news is that thinking strategies change as you age. Moreover, there is plenty you can do to express empathy politely and purposefully. To show empathy:

- Portray an active interest in their life by asking questions and keeping your attention focused on them. Avoid looking at your phone or looking elsewhere while they are speaking, as these actions indicate you are not really interested in what they are saying.
- Offer to help when someone is going through a tough time. There are many ways to show you care, including sending them a message, giving them a call, or offering to carry out a task.
- When you have an argument with someone, try to imagine how they feel or why they may have gotten upset. They may be going through a challenge at home and may need a little extra understanding.

5: *Learning how to Start, Maintain, and End a Conversation*

Teens, nowadays, use fewer "socialization muscles" than those from previous generations because they spend so much time on their phones and on social media (Morin, 2022). Conversation is an art, and you will probably find that the more you practice it, the better you get. You can start a conversation with a simple greeting; however, you can also start it with a compliment or a question.

Starting a conversation is not as difficult as maintaining one. The fear of awkward silence or oversharing might be stopping you from starting a conversation in the first place. Maybe you aren't confident enough or feel anxious while interacting. It's okay to feel all these emotions. But you should believe in yourself. You are who you are. Conversations with people around you will help you make new friends and strengthen those bonds. It's not necessary to continue a conversation and drag it out for an hour. A decent conversation can range from two minutes to more, depending on different situations.

To maintain a conversation, you can discuss things of mutual interest. In order to end a conversation, let the person know how much you enjoyed their company.

And that it was a pleasure being with them, and you would love to join them again soon. All such polite phrases can help you end a conversation without offending anyone.

6: Speaking Your Mind Assertively

Communication is about putting your point across and understanding others. How would you feel if someone doesn't take your opinion seriously? Despite how horrible it sounds; it can happen if you don't believe in yourself and don't have confidence in your stance. Being assertive and saying what you think, and feel is a sign of confidence and belief in yourself. Once you have confidence in yourself, everyone else will trust you. They will give you and your opinion its due value and importance. So, whenever you give a suggestion or express your point of view, be assertive (Being Assertive | Childline, n.d.).

Ask yourself what your communication style is. Do you prefer expressing yourself passively, aggressively, or assertively? When you present your opinions passively or aggressively, conveying your stance will become difficult. In the first case, a lack of self-confidence and faith in your opinion can cause it to be ignored. In the latter case, you might offend people, which can ultimately result in your opinion being neglected.

However, being assertive will demonstrate to others that you are confident and passionate about your belief, making them interested in what you say and more likely to listen to your opinions.

7: Knowing how to deal with Peer Pressure

As a teenager, peer pressure might be a daily part of your life. However, you may be surprised to learn that it isn't always a bad thing! For instance, your best friends and classmates may inspire you to get into reading books like the Harry Potter saga or The Hobbit, or they may motivate you to get physically active by practicing a sport alongside them.

Peer pressure is only harmful if it crosses your boundaries or leads you into unhealthy or self-destructive behaviors (Pontz, 2021). To deal with such kinds of peer pressure:

- Set your limits and confidently say "no" when someone tries to overstep them.
- Don't give long-winded explanations about why you can't do something. Instead, just say that you don't do it and leave it at that. For instance, "I don't mean to sound rude, but I don't meet up with people I connect with online." "I don't stay up longer than 11 pm." "I

don't drink alcohol." "I don't get into a vehicle if the driver has been drinking."

- Surround yourself with positive peer partners.
- Avoid situations that will make it difficult to resist peer pressure.

Communication is an essential skill needed in every aspect of life. It's not only about talking, but it's also about your behavior and body language. If you listen actively and understand others, you can solve many problems. In addition, if your body language radiates confidence and calmness, people will trust you with their care and value your opinion. You will be considered a responsible person.

In your home, communicating effectively with parents and siblings can help you understand them and make them know you. This will ultimately strengthen the bond you share with them. In your school, being polite and friendly will earn you long-lasting friendships. The art of starting, continuing, and ending a conversation plays a significant role in helping you socialize. A forward and assertive way of expressing yourself in social gatherings will help you gain others' trust. Moreover, controlling your emotions and staying calm during a conflict will add charm to your personality.

Now that you have aced the art of communication, you are ready to work on your confidence and resilience, so you can face peer pressure and other teen challenges with greater aplomb. So, turn the page and learn how you can evade difficult situations that can cause you serious problems.

2

SKILL TWO: REMAINING STRONG IN CHALLENGING TIMES

"Resilience is accepting your new reality, even if it's less good than the one you had before. You can fight it, you can do nothing but scream about what you've lost, or you can accept that and try to put together something that's good."

— *ELIZABETH EDWARDS*

One of the steps on the ladder that leads to success is knowing how to tackle failures. It is an integral life skill for anyone who wants to succeed. Starting from the time you begin to learn something new until you become proficient at it, you will face difficulties, hurdles, disappointments, and even failures. Knowing how to cope with them and the threat they can pose to your emotional and psychological health is essential. Because everyone experiences difficult times in their lives, but not everyone achieves what they struggle for.

Why is that so? The answer to this question is simple. Everyone has a different approach to difficult times and how to address them. And how someone handles difficult situations makes the difference in the long run.

Let's try to understand it with the following example.

Martin, Eric, and Theodore live in different regions of the world. Every one of them opens a flower shop. Unfortunately, their businesses have run at a loss for many consecutive months. Martin is highly disappointed and decides to sell his shop and quit the business. On the other hand, Eric considers the demographics and market research. Eventually, he concludes that the location of his store is causing a loss of business. He decides to switch the business, as he can't move to another location. Theodore evaluates the market trends, analyzes demographics and psychographics, and reviews his marketing strategies. He detects problems in his business strategies and solves them without delay. Moreover, he explores the strengths and weaknesses of his competitors and modifies his business accordingly. In the next few months, Theodore's flower shop achieves massive success.

In the above-mentioned example, you witnessed three different approaches to a single problem. The problem didn't determine the outcomes in any of these cases but the approach to addressing the problem produced the end results.

You might wonder what makes a person make the right decisions in difficult situations. There isn't any one specific trait but a group of attributes that a person can adopt over time, that can help them control their nerves in hard times and make appropriate decisions.

In your teenage years, you will face many issues just like everyone else your age. Some are burdened with lengthy syllabi while others are bullied at school. Some struggle with depression while many find it difficult to distance themselves from people with negative influences. A teen's life is very complicated, and the issues they face can be very serious.

The following are some of the most common problems teenagers face: (DeSilver, 2020)

- Stress
- Bullying
- Academic pressure

- Anxiety and depression
- Body image issues
- Peer pressure
- Social media
- On Screen violence

Failing to address problems adequately can be a huge mistake because unhappy experiences at this age can act as unhealed traumas that hold you back from giving your best in life (Lcsw, 2022).

BUILDING YOUR RESILIENCE

Resilience is the ability to recover, adapt, and bounce back from difficult life events. According to the American Psychological Association, it involves having the mental, emotional, and behavioral flexibility you need to make necessary adjustments. Resilience takes time to build, and it depends on other skills like self-esteem and communication skills, as well as the support you receive from those around you. Being resilient does not mean suppressing pain, fear, or stress. It involves working through these emotions and trying to find meaning in them while also creating a strategy to deal with the pitfalls.

The most interesting thing about resilience is that it includes toughness and flexibility. You might have heard about the analogy of a ship that sails in the ocean. It remains inside the ocean but doesn't sink if the water doesn't enter it. Similarly, problems are an important part of life to help you learn and grow. But when they start negatively affecting you, they become problematic. Being resilient brings that toughness inside you, enabling you to avoid being affected by things happening around you. At the same time, it inculcates flexibility inside you. This flexibility assists you in adapting to the changes.

If you remember some important principles of inertia, you know that changes in the state of matter are resisted. This can also be true in many situations in life. It is difficult for some people to accept changes. This rigid behavior creates problems for them. For example, with the emergence of AI, many people feared they would lose their jobs and didn't benefit from using the helpful features of artificial intelligence. Moreover, they suffered from stress and anxiety. On the other hand, those who viewed it as an advancement in technology and tried to adopt it were at an advantage.

Resilience allows people to view changes positively and change themselves accordingly. It is because changes of all types are an integral part of life. It can be difficult for a teen to adjust to a new school and make friends. They may also find it challenging to recover from a relationship breakup. All these, and many other changes, are a constant part of a teen's life. Therefore, learning how to build resilience can prove very important for you to make it through the thick and thin of this part of life (Teach Your Teenager to Be Resilient - ReachOut Parents, n.d.).

STRATEGIES FOR BUILDING RESILIENCE

Resilience cannot be built in a day or a month. It takes time and effort. So, how can you attain resilience at this age so that you can face almost every situation fearlessly? (Resilience in Pre-teens and Teenagers, 2021)

Buckle up! You are to start your journey toward learning the blockbuster skills you might have been dreaming of.

Embracing positive thinking habits

Let's say a swing is placed in the center of a park. People from all four sides of the park can see the swing. From all angles, it looks different. Similarly, for a paratrooper, the dimensions of the swing will be different from what those in the park can see. In short, both literally and metaphorically, there are many angles from which to view a certain thing. And oftentimes, we can choose between different points of view. So, whenever there is a problem, try to view all aspects of it. See if you can find something positive. Think positively about the situation that is causing you stress.

How you see a problem can make a huge difference. In order to think positively, you should first analyze the entire situation. It is because you should get to know the complete story before jumping to conclusions. Once everything is clear, you have to use the "What?" "Then?" and the "So" principle. When analyzing a situation, you should ask yourself:

"What is the problem I am facing at the moment?"

Next, you have to think about all the positive as well as negative aspects of the problem. Ask yourself:

"Then, what are the possible consequences?"

In this stage, you have to consider both the good and bad things that the problem can result in. Try to be positive and come up with the best possible solutions for this problem. Maybe it can help you learn something new or improve your ability. Maybe you found out about the issue early, or else it could have created a bigger mess. Whatever it is, think positively about it.

Finally, you have to solve the problem. It's time to ask yourself:

"What can I do to get out of this situation with little difficulty?"

Now, you have to think about all the possible solutions. You should remember that an issue can be addressed in more than one way. You should go for the solution that can actually put an end to the turmoil. Similarly, don't opt for shortcuts or temporary solutions.

For example, Amy and Adam have been criticizing Mark for his obesity. Casey has been observing this for many days. She tried to ignore it at first, but the way Mark has been sitting quietly at the end of class and staying alone all day, makes her feel bad. Now, she knows her "what?" The problem here is that Mark is being bullied by two classmates. Next, Casey thinks of the possible consequences of the problem, i.e., Mark's mental health is being badly affected. Finally, Casey has to find a solution. She can either ignore the situation completely or talk to Amy and Adam.

What do you think she should do?

Ignoring it is not a solution. And if Casey decides to talk to her classmates to ask them to stop attacking Mark, they may treat her similarly. The safest option is to talk to the teacher or student counselor. Casey should not think of it as complaining against Amy and Adam; but she is doing it for everyone's betterment. She should, then, behave nicely with both parties.

Becoming your own friend

Many people rely on their friends for emotional and moral support. Whatever the circumstances, they can share their problem with their friends and ask them for suggestions. Having someone listen to you can be comforting if you are going through difficult times. Just like that, you lend an empathetic ear to your friends when they need you.

What if you become that source of emotional and moral support for yourself? This doesn't mean you don't have to reach out for help when you need it. It simply means that you should develop self-love and use it to pull yourself together, console yourself, motivate yourself, and become your own strength. This is because you could encounter something stressful and might not have anyone around to help you control your nerves. You will have to do it on your own. You will have to become your own friend and tell yourself, "It's alright!"

By simply knowing that stress isn't good for your psychological health, you will try to detach yourself from negativity and will be able to help yourself understand that no matter what the issue is, it won't last forever. Neither will its side effects. And by no means is it more important than your mental well-being.

You will then be able to encourage yourself and inculcate positive energy so that you can solve the problem. You can fix things, and it's okay to make mistakes. Everyone makes mistakes, and everyone fails. But not everyone realizes that failure is a constant part of life, accepts the failure, and learns from it. Remember, your mistakes never define you. The way you rectify them and learn from them is what is important.

Let's say Sarah has to perform a song on stage at school. The noise of the crowd overwhelms her. She is nervous and afraid of performing in front of so many people, and she is experiencing severe stress and anxiety. When her performance is just a few minutes away, she decides to calm herself down with positive self-talk. "It's alright, Sarah. It's okay to be nervous before such a huge performance. But you don't have to worry about anything. You have practiced a lot, and trust me, you will do great. Believe in yourself. You will nail it." After having this conversation with herself, Sarah feels a lot better and performs confidently on the stage. Her performance wasn't affected by the anxiety, and the audience burst into applause as soon as she ended her song.

Have a broader point of view

You might have seen people around you stressing over little things. Not achieving certain goals disappoints them badly. They become depressed. Because they don't achieve success in the first few tries, they start believing that they can't do it no matter what, and therefore they stop trying. This view must be changed. To build resilience, you need to believe that no matter what happens, it is not the end of the world!

Imagine there is a line drawn on a page with different dots along its length. Some dots are blue, others are orange. Imagine these blue dots as happy moments in your life and the orange dots as sad ones. After every dot comes another one. It can be good or bad. Even after consecutive orange dots, you will get to those blue dots. Every single problem will fade away with time. Now, you have to decide how you will use this time to react to that problem and tackle it.

Know that there's a whole life ahead of you to live. Failing to achieve something easily does not mean you can never achieve it. It simply means that you need more practice. You need to work more. When you start viewing your failure as a small dot on the timeline of your life, you will worry less about it. Because you know you will get better opportunities, or maybe you will create opportunities for yourself. Don't get upset or depressed. Don't hold onto that failure and the hurt it brings. Being sad about not getting something you worked for is not wrong but adding it to your emotional baggage is. Let the feelings and emotions come and leave you unharmed.

Let's say Eva had been playing basketball since she was young. She practiced and practiced. But her team never wins the final tournament. She tells herself that she isn't capable of winning, and if she loses one more time, she will quit the sport.

Now pause for a second and try to find what's problematic with what she's doing. First, she has been holding onto previous failures. Second, she is piling up failures in her subconscious. Third, she is looking at her future through the lens of past failures.

Unfortunately, Eva's team loses the final tournament again. After entering her home, she locks herself in her room and cries. She stops talking to family members, friends, and teammates. She quits the sport and tries things she isn't interested in.

So, what did she gain and what did she lose?

Eva has lost her years-long struggle to learn to play basketball. She has let failure impact her entire life. She gained a lot of heartache and bad memories. If Eva had spent more time training with her teammates, she could have had a better chance of winning the final tournament.

Build and enhance self-confidence

Believing in yourself and having self-confidence is a powerful tool that empowers you to do extraordinary things. This can help you thrive personally and professionally by creating opportunities that may seem out of reach. A great example of this is demonstrated in the story of the farmer's self-belief below.

Once, there was a farmer. He moved from place to place and worked on other people's farms to make a living. One day he went to a village that was named "The Barren Valley". It was named so because of the barren land that didn't support the growth of crops. Even if the crops grew, the pests in the area destroyed the entire field. This was the reason people continued migrating from the place until the village shrank to a handful of houses. The farmer was interested in experimenting with the soil of the barren valley; therefore, he started living in the village.

Days and months passed until, finally, a year had gone by. The farmer continued to work. People laughed at him, but he didn't pay attention to any gossip. Finally, he raised crops and succeeded in protecting them from pests.

Everyone was shocked. Those who used to laugh at him asked, "Why did you continue trying despite knowing that no one ever succeeded in growing crops here since the pests overtook the fields?"

The farmer smiled and said, "All those who failed were not me. I am a different individual with my own capabilities. And I believe in them."

Another villager posed a question, "But you failed several times, why didn't you stop trying?"

"It is because there are a million ways of doing things, and I have not tried all of them yet. I kept trying until one of them worked, and I got the most beautiful results."

Self-confidence teaches you resilience. Just as the farmer believed in his abilities and kept working despite continuous failures, self-confidence induces toughness inside you. Moreover, the way the farmer tried new strategies every time shows his flexible behavior. He did not continue doing ineffective things: rather, he innovated and evolved.

How much others trust your abilities does matter, but your trust in yourself holds significant importance. In difficult times, if you have that faith and belief in yourself, you will make it out of difficult situations without much stress or anxiety. Imagine there's someone you trust the most. If some problem occurs in their presence, you don't panic at all because you know you are covered. That's what self-confidence does to a person in the face of difficulties. You can simply tell yourself, "I know I will figure it out." (biglifejournal.com, n.d.).

In addition, if you have self-confidence, no matter what others say about you, it won't disturb your psychological condition. For Example, Alice got a new haircut. She was happy to show it to her friends. When her friends saw her new hairstyle, they laughed at her and told her how funny she looked. Alice valued their opinion over her own and got depressed. She couldn't get her old hair back, but she couldn't enjoy the new one she had wanted for so long. She ended up hating her hairstyle.

If Alice had self-confidence, she could have stood by her choice. The haircut was her choice, and no one can make fun of it. Even if they do, she should not have cared. But her lack of belief in herself made her suffer from emotional turmoil.

Building a solid support system

From time to time, we need help from people around us. It can be assistance with material tasks or in the form of suggestions and moral support. Building a strong support system is extremely helpful in life. As a teen, you might encounter problems you can't handle alone. In such situations, sharing the issue with a family member or a trusted friend can prove to be the best approach. Though there are many things you can handle by yourself, asking for help or advice, in some cases, is crucial.

Building solid friendships and relationships can be a critical source of support when things get tough. This habit will also help you when you need serious advice or help later in your professional life.

Exactly how can your support system help you?

Example: Michael was stuck in a bad peer group that encouraged him to indulge in nuisance. First, he misbehaved with his parents and disobeyed them. Second, he left all his old friends to adjust to his new friends. Then he did everything his new friends asked him to do. Shockingly, he even started using drugs, and slowly, gradually, his dependence on drugs increased. His condition worsened, but his friends didn't seem to understand his problems. Eventually, he decided to reach out for help. But he had cut himself off from everyone in his friend circle. He had let down his parents and was hesitant in sharing his problems with them. Consequently, he went through the worst times and ended up in the hospital.

Had he chosen the right people or strengthened the bond with his parents and friends, he could have shared it with any of them. Indeed, many issues can't be shared with just anyone. You need some very close and trustworthy people in your life, to reach out to, whenever you find the need for it.

EMBRACING THE GROWTH MINDSET

Having a growth mindset is another key element of resilience. With this mindset, you persevere when challenged, learn from failure, make great efforts to achieve your goals and value a positive attitude. You also know that you can learn anything you want to. You celebrate others' success. You love being told that you try hard.

When you favor a fixed mindset, you give up when you are frustrated, judge yourself when you fail, feel threatened by others' success, and believe that innate abilities, rather than effort and determination, impact the outcome. You need validation from others; you like it when they acknowledge you are smart.

To succeed at anything in life. One should understand that a successful life demands growth. Think of a science book in your grandfather's library that has been there for years. You will find a massive difference after comparing it to the facts of science and technology today. You will observe how things have evolved and how theories have been modified. Some principles have been used as the basis for modern advancements, etc. In short, life is all about learning and growing. And a successful life requires a growth mindset.

As discussed above, there are two major types of mind-sets, i.e., the fixed mindset and the growth mindset.

The characteristics of a person with a fixed mindset are the following:

- A person with a fixed mindset will think negatively.
- To them, any difficulty in life is either because of fate or because of others.
- People with this mindset blame others for their failures and miserable state.
- They never take responsibility for their actions.
- They tell themselves that it's misfortune and not a lack of hard work that prevents them from succeeding.
- They don't expect good things from the future.
- They feel envy when others succeed.
- They gossip about others.
- They try to pull others down.
- They become unhappy when they see others happy.
- They opt for shortcuts.
- They avoid hard work and challenges.

- They don't take risks.
- They expect results without putting in effort.
- They hate constructive criticism and feedback on things they lack.
- They don't accept mistakes.
- They do not accept that people can be better than them.
- They think they can do everything on their own.

All these things make them fall behind in the race of life. On the other hand, the person with a growth mindset has a broad mind and is flexible enough to incorporate changes into their life.

The characteristics of people with a growth mindset are as follows:

- They think positively and focus on the positive aspects of life.
- They believe in themselves and their capabilities.
- They take responsibility for their actions and never blame others.
- They have a positive outlook on life. If something bad happens to them, they try to overcome it as soon as they can.
- They look forward to a bright future.

- They are happy to see others succeed.
- They never take part in gossip.
- They teach others everything they know and help them succeed.
- They are happy to see others happy.
- They don't like shortcuts. Instead, they calculate everything and invest time and energy in the areas of life that can benefit them in the long run.
- They work hard and accept challenges bravely.
- They take measured risks.
- They put all their energy into making efforts.
- They appreciate constructive criticism and welcome the feedback provided to improve themselves.
- They accept their mistakes and try to learn from them.
- They believe that other people can have better knowledge and skills than them and are always ready to learn.
- They never hesitate to ask for help.

Activity

Now that you know the difference between a growth mindset and a fixed mindset, here's an interesting activity for you. Write down examples of growth and fixed mindsets. The first example has been written for you.

FIXED MINDSET	GROWTH MINDSET
I got a C on my math test. I'll never succeed at math. I might as well stop studying for the tests and take it as a sure failure.	I got a C on my math test. I will examine my errors and practice the areas I made mistakes in.

BUILDING SELF-ESTEEM AND REFRAMING NEGATIVE BELIEFS

Self-esteem is all about how you see yourself and people around you. For example, Julian is such a nice person. Lily is the brightest student in her class. Gorge is cooperative. Hannah's communication skills are implacable. David is a science geek, and so on. In short, the way you have your overall view of someone, of how good or bad they are as an individual, or how intelligent and capable they are, you also have an opinion of yourself (Self-esteem and Self-confidence, 2019).

Take a moment and think about your image of yourself. This belief you have about yourself is your self-esteem. If you have a positive self-image, building resilience will be easy for you. However, if you have a negative self-image and think you can't do things, staying strong in the face of challenges will be difficult.

To build self-esteem, you must first get rid of negative beliefs. Therefore, you should try to reframe how you see yourself and the situations you face in life. Everything that happens to you has a purpose. Success boosts your confidence, whereas failures prepare you for success. Deriving meaning from life experiences is everyone's own choice. Though some factors may influence your perception of these occurrences, i.e., past experiences brought up, fear and phobias, self-esteem, etc. Despite this, individuals can derive positive or negative meanings from different incidents.

Unfortunately, most teenagers have low self-esteem. They tell themselves, "I am not good enough" or "I don't deserve to be successful."

What are the causes of low self-esteem in teens?

Firstly, how parents raise their children, treat them, and react to their achievements and failures is vital in building their children's self-esteem. If your parents encourage and support you, you will likely have a positive self-image. On the other hand, if they fail to understand your positive intentions and keep reminding you of your mistakes, you might suffer from low self-esteem. This happens because the opinions of people who matter to you are significant in forming your view of yourself.

In general, the prime cause of low self-esteem is the treatment an individual receives from people around them. Moreover, the more knowledge and skills they have, the better they will feel about themselves.

On the other hand, if they have little knowledge, they might consider themselves inferior to others. Another prominent cause of low self-esteem is the raised standards of success and happiness presented by social media. Besides, challenges and stressful experiences in life can result in a negative self-image.

You can leave the bitter experiences behind and start feeling good about yourself by practicing compassion towards yourself. By taking care of your physical and psychological well-being, you are very much likely to overcome a negative self-image. Work on the following tips to build strong self-esteem:

- Read books and gain knowledge of different fields of life.
- Learn small skills like making your bed properly, cleaning your room, organizing your wardrobe, cooking easy dishes, making a salad, solving Rubik's cube, providing first aid, using fire extinguishers, etc.
- Exercise regularly.
- Eat well.
- Take a proper 6-8 hours of sleep.
- Take part in sports.
- Meditate.
- Write down your thoughts in a diary and write five motivational sentences praising yourself every day.
- Say positive affirmations regularly.
- Accept challenges. Try things out of your comfort zone.
- Smile more often.
- Learn to enjoy your time with people and without them.
- Make new friends.

Building self-esteem isn't completely possible unless you leave behind all the negative views about yourself. Negative beliefs about oneself can form over a lifetime, contributing to low self-esteem. To get rid of negative beliefs, start working on your mindset. Replace negative thoughts with positive ones by observing your thoughts and reframing the negative thoughts. You can practice saying the following ones:

- I can do it.
- I am improving and one day I will succeed.
- I can learn anything by working on it.
- I deserve love and appreciation.
- I love myself.

Saying positive affirmations to yourself is one way of leaving negative beliefs behind. The other way is by changing the negative thought into a positive one right away. For example, if you catch yourself thinking poorly of your life, turn that negative statement into a positive one (Helping Children Reframe Negative Thoughts: Mentally Healthy Schools, n.d.).

The table below shows some examples of how you can do it.

SITUATION	NEGATIVE THOUGHTS OR BELIEFS	EVIDENCE AGAINST THIS	REFRAME
Sonya didn't choose me for the group project in class.	Everyone hates me and thinks I'm dumb.	Dylan, who is really bright and good at science, chose me to be in his group.	Being in a group with new people enabled me to get closer to classmates I previously didn't talk to much. I also discovered how smart and funny many of them are.
I failed the Math test.	I am not intelligent.	I scored excellent in science.	Not being good at one subject doesn't mean that I am not intelligent. I can work a little more and will ace the next Maths test for sure.
Ryle can play guitar and knows how to cook. Everyone likes him.	He is far better than me at everything.	I can solve a Rubik's cube in less than a minute.	Ryle might be good at many things, so am I. I should not compare myself to anyone because everyone has their own life and a different meaning of success.
After the tryouts the coach did not select me in the basketball team.	I am not good at playing basketball.	In my previous school, I was a member of the school basketball team for five consecutive years.	Out of many students, the coach could only add two new players to the team. He chose the best players. This doesn't mean I am not good at playing basketball. It simply means I should continue practicing.

For you to persevere in the face of challenges, you must have confidence in yourself and your abilities. Resilience is an important life skill that, if learned in your teenage years, can help you live a successful life.

To build resilience, you should try to adopt a positive and growth mindset. You should console yourself and motivate yourself. By doing so, you will be able to control your nerves better and find the best possible solution to the problems.

Once you have worked on important areas like resilience and reframing negative self-beliefs, you can tackle two skills that people of all ages sometimes find difficult to achieve: time management and problem-solving! These are the skills that made entrepreneurs like Elon Musk, Mark Zuckerberg, and Steve Jobs what they are today. So, turn the page and discover the skills that can lead you to success.

3

SKILL THREE: USING TIME WISELY AND BEING AN EFFICIENT PROBLEM SOLVER

"The most efficient way to live reasonably is every morning to make a plan of one's day and every night to examine the results obtained."

— *ALEXIS CARREL*

D o you know that 80% of people don't have a dedicated time management system? (Time Management Statistics - 2023 | 99firms, n.d.)

Statistics have shown that teens who can manage their time successfully are less stressed as compared to those who can't (10 Surprising Facts About Teens and Time Management, n.d.). It is because a teen's life is jam-packed with quite a lot of activities, and each one of them is important in forming habits that will impact their personality in a positive manner. For example, exercising, playing sports, learning to play a musical instrument, learning to cook, socializing, studying, etc.

Not being able to manage your time can cause many issues. When you fail to allocate proper time to all these activities, you won't be able to focus on any of them. While you will be busy doing one thing, you might start thinking about the next task, and, this way, both tasks will remain incomplete.

It has been scientifically proven that multitasking (doing various things at once instead of concentrating on one of them) reduces your productivity by up to 45% (10 Surprising Facts About Teens and Time Management, n.d.). For this purpose, segregating the tasks from one another, spending the right amount of time on them, and focusing on one task at a time can be extremely helpful. However, doing all these things requires you to manage your time.

On a scale from one to ten, rank yourself on how good you are at time management. One implies extremely poor time management, while ten shows excellent time management.

Do you want to become better at managing your time?

This chapter will show you effective strategies to help you manage your time wisely. Moreover, you will learn to solve different problems you might encounter in your everyday life as a teenager. Without any further ado, let's learn these interesting skills!

STRATEGIES FOR USING TIME WISELY

Time is a valuable resource; the time you spend studying, playing sports, or hanging out with friends is utilized at the expense of other productive activities you could be doing. The decision about how you spend your time should be well thought out if you wish to achieve your goals. Here are some efficient strategies to help you hone your time management skills:

1: Write down all the things you must do in a typical day

Your list might include things like studying, reading, working out, playing computer games, having a snack, having dinner, taking a shower, performing relaxation exercises before going to bed, etc. Daily activities of individuals can vary, however most of them are basically the same. You can write down things you have to do every day.

The nature of these tasks can differ, depending on time, i.e., some tasks must be done at a certain time while others can be done at any time of the day. Write "rigid" against all such tasks that have to be done at a specific time. Then, write "flexible" against activities that can be performed anytime in a day.

Next, you have to set your priorities. Of all the tasks you have listed, which are the most important ones? Separate them from the rest of the tasks. If it's your study or your daily workout, etc., just mark them as important. Setting priorities will help you cater to any spontaneous tasks that arise that are not included in your schedule. You will be taught to address such unplanned events later in this chapter.

Now, it's time to put these activities into a schedule and aim to follow this schedule strictly so that you do not miss out on essential activities.

Scheduling

Scheduling is not as complicated as it might sound. It is an interesting activity and helps you stay organized. A schedule usually comprises the tasks of your day along with the time they might require. Your schedule may also include the exact time of day you are supposed to complete the task.

While preparing your schedule, you should keep in mind that your activities on weekdays can differ from those on weekends. So, you might need two different schedules, i.e., one for the working days and the other for weekends. In order to make a single schedule for all the days of the week, take a sheet of paper, a paper journal, or an online journal, and follow the steps mentioned below:

- Write down the 24 hours of the day, starting from the time you wake up.
- Write the "rigid" tasks against the hours of the day they must be completed. This can include taking a shower early in the morning.
- Now you can put the rest of the tasks on your schedule while keeping in mind the time of the

day when you can get them done more productively.

- Let's say that self-study sessions are flexible tasks that can be placed anywhere on your schedule. So, you can choose the time of day when you are most energetic. For example, on weekends, after you work out in the morning, take a shower, and have your breakfast, you can schedule a self-study session.

- Do the same with all the remaining tasks, i.e., think of what time is best for doing them.

- You had previously marked some tasks as important while setting your priorities. Highlight these tasks with a red color. The reason for doing it is that you should know you cannot skip these except in case of emergency.

- Highlight the activities that can be skipped if an unplanned event occurs with a yellow color. However, these activities should not be skipped for two consecutive days.

- Lastly, highlight the least important activities with a green color, that can be skipped anytime for any number of days, if something important comes up.

So, what are the characteristics of a good schedule?

You have observed a general method of scheduling, but before you start scheduling your days, consider the following do's and don'ts:

- Your timetable/schedule should be flexible enough to accommodate unexpected events or tasks.
- Do not try to copy a timetable from your favorite celebrity or influencer, as it might prove to be extremely unrealistic for you. For example, adding 2 hours of workout to your schedule suddenly will drain your energy, and you will ultimately leave your timetable.
- It should be easy to implement.
- It should have proper time allocated to self-care.
- It should contain six to eight hours of sleep.
- It should not have difficult tasks piled up one after another. Rather, two difficult tasks should be separated by an easy, interesting, and refreshing activity.
- You can also adjust small 15–20-minute breaks are important.

How to make yourself follow the schedule?

You won't be shocked to know that out of all the people who prepare schedules and planners, very few can implement them or get the tasks done.

Why is it so? It is because things are easier said than done, and the fact that most people set unrealistic goals while scheduling makes them exhausted quickly. Therefore, they leave tasks unaccomplished and are demotivated and discouraged. They start believing that making schedules or planners is of no use. That's not entirely false.

Planners cannot benefit those who hesitate to work hard and stay in search of shortcuts. Because schedules are just the guiding perimeters. It is your actions that bring these plans to reality. It takes the following attributes to manage time successfully when using a planner:

- Will to implement the tasks
- Hard Work
- Consistency
- Commitment
- Resilience

First and foremost, your intentions to start a task, make it a part of your daily routine, and continue it matters the most. If you want to implement it on your schedule and wish to gain benefits from it, you have climbed the first step of the ladder.

Next comes the stage of consistent hard work. Doing the task little by little every single day and not missing it, whether you feel like doing it or not, is what this stage demands. Tell yourself, "Do it anyway!" and simply get started. Little efforts made every day can give huge results. Doing all these tasks that require days and months in one day is neither possible nor beneficial.

Think of working regularly as if you are connecting links to form a long chain. You can only add one link to your chain in a day, no matter if you do something for 4 hours or half an hour a day. Working regularly will help you build a long chain. It is called consistency. When you continue doing something at regular intervals, you are practicing consistency. It's a very important personality trait that can help you learn and master several skills.

Commitment is giving your word to do something. You need to commit to your schedule in order to follow it and benefit from it. This commitment doesn't have to be for a year. Make small agreements with yourself. Let's say you agree to follow your schedule for two days. After you accomplish this target, set a little bigger one. Make an agreement to implement it on your planner for five days, and slowly you can increase the number of days. Remember to set achievable goals.

You will most likely face some difficulties when following the planner. Your resilience will help you tackle these problems and get things done. Don't panic or get upset. Try to relax and take a break when things go wrong. Gather your strength by motivating yourself, observing your thoughts and thinking positively.

For example, it was Max's study time, but his relatives were visiting. The entire house was a mess as children were playing, running around, and making noise. He was controlling his anger when, finally, he decided to take a deep breath, picked his books and other study essentials, and left for the library. This way, he was able to control his anger and focus on his studies.

Adjusting unplanned events in your schedule

Though it sounds annoying, this problem is inevitable. From time to time, things you haven't prepared for in your schedule will come up and test your patience. They can lead you to fail in the implementation of your timetable. This problem can be solved to some extent by comparing the tasks from your schedule with the unscheduled task. Ask yourself the following questions:

- Which activity is important?
- Which activity can be done later?
- What are the consequences of neglecting the unscheduled task?
- What consequences can I face by skipping scheduled tasks?
- If I go and complete the unplanned task, when can I possibly complete the scheduled task?

Analyze the answers to these questions carefully, and then make your decision.

Complete a task in its allocated time

Let's say you have designed your schedule. How can you ensure that every task is completed in its assigned time? Here are some tips to get it done:

- Get rid of distractions. The very first thing you have to do is remove all the possible distractions within your sight. Whether it's a musical instrument, sports equipment, or an electronic gadget, keep them away while you are focusing on your task, like studying.
- Maintain focus. We tend to think all the time. You cannot stop your brain from thinking. But this function of the brain can hinder the completion of your task. To avoid it, you should

be mindful of the thoughts that enter your mind. If you find yourself taking interest in any of the thoughts, redirect your focus to your work.

- Say no to multitasking. Don't do more than one thing at a time because this can increase the possibility of one or both activities staying unaccomplished and flawed.

- Actively engage with the task. Don't just do something because it's written on your schedule. Do it properly. Take an interest in it.

One of the most important tasks that you might need to do every day as a teen is studying. Here are some tips to help you manage your time to become strong in academics.

Set study goals and plan for them

Is it a good idea to open a random page of your book and start studying whatever comes in front of you? Of course not. You won't get to know the background of certain topics. There won't be a proper foundation to store new knowledge. And you might easily forget it. To avoid this inconvenience, you should plan and set study goals. You can set daily, weekly, and monthly goals to help you prepare well before exams.

Slow and steady wins the race

Instead of waiting for the week before your exams to study, start studying at the beginning of the school term. Use a weekly planner to set aside specific days and times for each subject. Study all the courses/subjects little by little every day. If you find it difficult, ask your teachers or friends to help you.

PREPARATION FOR EXAMS

Do you feel overworked or excessively burdened just before exams?

Not studying regularly can make preparation for exams difficult. Try to study every day. Around three weeks before exams, work out how much you must learn (divide each subject into a specific number of chapters, pages, or topics). Commit to studying a set number of these per day. Leave a few days at the end just for revision.

The following section will guide you to study in an efficient manner.

Effective learning techniques

Use study aids like mnemonics, mind maps, cards, and similar things. SimpleMind is an app that helps you organize your thoughts by creating mind maps. Oftentimes, the information is very similar and seems to jumble up in the mind. Mnemonic techniques can help you memorize things without difficulty. They make the study material interesting and easy to remember.

Reward yourself

Reward yourself for sticking to your routine. Include breaks, meet-ups with friends, and social networking, knowing that during the exam period, the time you dedicate to these activities may be a little shorter than usual. It is very important that you reward yourself for your efforts, hard work, and consistency.

Create a Study-Friendly Space

The design of your study area has a big effect on your ability to revise successfully. Ensure your space is:

- Organized and tidy. When it is time to study or read, choose a quiet, appealing spot. Make sure your desk is well-organized since clutter can interfere with your ability to concentrate.
- Quiet and personal. Having your siblings and/or parents around while you study can be a distraction.
- Filled with natural light. Sunlight boosts your mood, lessens anxiety, and improves your productivity.
- Ergonomic. Make sure your computer is at the right distance from your eyes, that you have an adjustable seat, and that your feet are flat on the floor or supported by a footrest.
- Plants purify the air, reduce stress levels, and boost your productivity.

ONLINE TIME MANAGEMENT TOOLS FOR TEENS

There are many online tools out there that can help you save time, keep a check on where you spend your time, schedule your days, prepare to-do lists, and help you effectively implement them. Some of these beneficial tools are mentioned below: (Scoro & Scoro, 2022)

Remember the Milk

It is an important mobile app that both Android and iPhone users can use. It helps you manage your tasks by making to-do lists and schedules. You can also mark essential tasks as priorities. Remember the Milk will save your tasks with dates and deadlines and remind you of things that need to be done.

Evernote

Evernote is a note-taking app you can access from all your devices, including Windows, iOS, Mac, Android, etc. If a pending task comes to your mind while you are busy, you can write it in Evernote to work on it later. You can also write down important points while you study to revise them whenever you want. Moreover, you can write down your thoughts and use Evernote as a journal.

Offtime

If you can easily be distracted by social media apps while using your phone for some productive work, Offtime can be your best solution. It can be used on both iPhone and Android. It calculates your time on different apps and helps you customize which apps you can use in different parts of the day. You can also mention your working hours so the app can block the use of other distractive apps during those hours.

Streaks

Streaks is an Apple-friendly app that helps you make to-do lists. It will keep a record of your tasks in the form of streaks. If you complete the tasks regularly, the streaks will grow. Skipping the task will break the streak, and you must start again. This app can help you learn new skills and good habits (STREAKS. the To-do List That Helps You Form Good Habits. For iOS., n.d.).

Being able to manage your time can help you become more productive. This will benefit you in your everyday life, and it can be highly advantageous in the long run. Time management is just one of the issues that teens face.

You have learned some strategies for managing your time. However, the list doesn't end here. There are countless other issues that can arise and hinder your progress. Learning to solve them will reduce stress and boost your confidence. Here are some exceptional tips to teach you how to solve such problems.

SOLVE PROBLEMS WITH A RESULTS-BASED APPROACH

When a problem arises, you have two choices. One is to focus on the unfairness of the situation by getting upset, frustrated, or angry. It is okay to have these feelings, but spending too much time on them can be counterproductive. The second choice is to accept your thoughts and feelings about the situation, solve the problem, and move on (Shameer, 2023).

Problem-solving has a series of steps you should follow. You may not always obtain the results you want the first time around, but if a strategy doesn't work out, know that there are other approaches you can try in the future. Successful problem-solving involves:

- Identifying the problem
- Identifying different solutions
- Choosing a solution
- Executing the solution
- Analyzing your problem-solving strategy by journaling
- Learning from failures

Identify the problem

Identifying the problem is the first step towards solving it. For instance, the issue might be a project you are working on, and you need Photoshop for the design element of your work. However, your computer at home doesn't have Photoshop. Your problem may also be more social in nature. For instance, you might be throwing a party, and your parents may have told you that you can only invite six people. However, you suddenly remember you forgot to invite your friend Rina from dance class—and she knows other people who will be at your party!

Identify various solutions

In the first example, solutions might include:

- Asking your parents to take you to a friend's house who has a computer with Photoshop.
- Asking your parents to pay for a Photoshop plan since you use this program frequently for school and this problem is likely to arise in the future.
- Using an alternative program to edit your images.

In the second example, solutions might include:

- Asking your parents if you can invite one more person, explaining that Rina is important to you and that she might get hurt if you leave her out.
- Make another plan with Rina to celebrate your birthday—for instance, inviting her to lunch and the movies on the weekend.

- Having another party that involves less expense per person, so you can increase your guest list.

Choosing one solution

Weigh the pros and cons of each possible solution. You can also consider a solution that is the most convenient. Also, think of everything you might need to do to execute that plan. Don't forget to keep a backup solution in mind in case your chosen solution doesn't work. After you have chosen which solution to go for, execute it.

Analyze the strategy you chose

Use a journal to analyze the success of your chosen solution. Write down the results of your problem-solving journey. If things didn't go as well as you would have liked, identify another solution that might have worked better for future reference.

Learn from failures

See failures as an opportunity for growth. Failure is the best teacher you will ever have in your life. Celebrate the lessons failure has taught you about yourself and others. Learn about your weaknesses and work on them to convert them into your strengths.

Life will send several challenges your way but remember that they are there to make you stronger. Sometimes it's essential to leave your comfort zone to understand life's lessons. Ups and downs are part of a successful life. No one has a perfect life. Everyone faces problems and difficulties, though the nature of these difficulties might be different. But what makes the difference is how you react and sort out the issue. All the successful figures that the world has known were excellent problem solvers. They didn't panic when a problem arose. They simply accepted challenges or took a break to steady their nerves. Then they used both their intellect and emotions to find solutions.

Finding solutions is, however, not an easy task. Sometimes you can figure it out within minutes, while it can also take days for you to find the right solution. Just remember that it's okay if you aren't able to find a solution immediately. Don't stress yourself; instead, keep working on the problem to see if you missed something important that could lead you to find a solution.

In this chapter, you learned how to manage time effectively by making schedules and successfully executing them. You can accomplish huge goals by taking one small step at a time. Execute a small part of your task every day and practice consistency. Do not procrastinate, as it can affect your willpower to follow your planner. Don't overthink; rather, focus on one part of your day at a time and focus on one task. Doing things with consistency and dedication will give you the strength to learn a new habit or a skill.

Now that you are an ultra-efficient time manager and problem-solver, it's time to take your game to the next level and work on something that many people neglect in their daily lives: their physical and mental health!

4

SKILL FOUR: PRIORITIZING YOUR PHYSICAL AND MENTAL HEALTH

"Health is a state of complete mental, social and physical well-being, not merely the absence of disease or infirmity."

— *WORLD HEALTH ORGANIZATION*

As you get older, you become more occupied by different activities. These activities will not leave you with enough time to take care of your mental and physical health if you haven't already set the habit. Many individuals neglect their health because, to them, the rest of their activities are more important. For example, some students think nothing holds more importance in their lives than their academic success and studies. All such causes can lead them to ignore their well-being.

Why do they behave this way?

Humans are always searching for instant and immediate results. For example, students get to see their grades after taking a test. However, spending time on your physical and mental health might not pay off instantly, but keeping good health will improve the quality of your life. Unfortunately, most individuals focus on things that can provide immediate results instead of investing time in long-term self-care.

Consequently, they become more likely to suffer from severe physical and psychological disorders. By the time they realize how unfair they have been to themselves, it's too late. They go through physical pain. In many cases, their organs cannot function properly, or they catch diseases quickly. Moreover, their immune system keeps weakening (Why Is Sleep Important? | NHLBI, NIH, 2022).

If you neglect your psychological health and work under extreme stress, turn a blind eye to your anxiety, suppress your depression, and refuse to seek help, you might develop serious health issues, i.e., chronic depression, etc. Always remember that nothing is more important than a person's health. It is because when health is compromised, it can affect a person's entire life. Therefore, you need to take the right steps, from this very moment onward, to dedicate a small part of your day to taking care of your mental and physical health. As prevention is better than cure.

Do you know that three out of four teens aren't getting enough exercise? (75% of Teens Aren't Getting Recommended Daily Exercise: New Study Suggests Supportive School Environment Is Linked to Higher Physical Activity Levels, 2022). Being inactive contributes to obesity, but it can also deprive teens of a vital means to battle stress, anxiety, and depression. Statistics have also unveiled the concerning fact that tweens and teens aged twelve to nineteen have worse diets than those aged six to eleven, and five and under. (National Study Finds Diets Remain Poor for Most American Children; Disparities Persist, 2020)

Moreover, stress among teens is on the rise. An American Psychological Association survey showed that teens report their stress levels are higher than what they believe to be healthy (Children's Resource Group, 2019).

In past chapters, we spoke of the many challenges teens are facing and the changes that their brains and bodies undergo during this unique time in life. Consider working out, eating healthily, and curbing stress as powerful tools that can help you overcome challenges, fulfill your obligations, and be the very best version of yourself possible.

Participating in extracurricular activities and sports that involve physical activity can improve your health. It can have many benefits that you might not know about. Let's learn about them.

BEING PHYSICALLY ACTIVE

Physical activities such as brisk walking, running, etc., are extremely beneficial for your health. (Youth Physical Activity Guidelines | Physical Activity | Healthy Schools | CDC, n.d.) Firstly, they help strengthen your bones as they are weight-bearing activities. When bones bear more than usual weight, it stimulates bone cells to grow, divide, and form new tissues. Moreover, bone density increases as the body prepares the bones to bear extra weight. The mineral content of bones increases, making them stronger. This reduces the risk of osteoporosis, a bone disease characterized by weak and brittle bones.

In addition, physical activities regulate the hormones of the endocrine system to initiate functions of different cells, tissues, and organs of the body. Somatotropic hormone, or somatotropin, is responsible for human growth. Its secretion in blood results in the development of an individual. Physical activities like exercising, jogging, cycling, etc., stimulate its secretion. Moreover, exercising stimulates the secretion of dopamine, which is a neurotransmitter as well as a hormone. It is responsible for happiness, satisfaction, pleasure, motivation, and many other emotions. It plays a significant role in humans' physical and psychological well-being (Depression and Anxiety: Exercise Eases Symptoms, 2017b).

Additionally, hormones like epinephrine, norepinephrine, and cortisol increase during exercise and return to normal after rest. Epinephrine and cortisol hormones prepare the body to cope with unusual or emergencies by increasing the blood pressure, respiration rate, metabolic rate, etc. Norepinephrine normalizes all changes after the situation becomes normal. These hormones are essential for the human body to survive shocking or stressful situations (Exercise Endocrine System Interaction, n.d.).

Exercising also makes one's body relatively more insulin sensitive. Insulin is a hormone that regulates blood glucose levels by reducing glucose in the blood. It works antagonistically with glucagon, which increases blood glucose levels when they're low to maintain them. When insulin is secreted in less than-average amounts, it results in diabetes mellitus. When a person exercises, their body becomes sensitive to insulin, which means their blood glucose level can be decreased to normal with little insulin (Preventing Diabetes, n.d.).

Finally, exercising regulates the secretion of reproductive hormones, i.e., luteinizing hormones, estrogen, testosterone, etc. LH is responsible for ovulation in the female reproductive system. Enhanced secretions of the hormones mentioned above can improve fertility. Exercise has many more benefits, with research showing that it can improve cognitive function for youths, reduce the risk of cancer, improve brain health, promote healthier sleep patterns, and improve your quality of life (Whyte, 2021).

Therefore, teens and adolescents aged six to seventeen need one hour or more of moderate-to-vigorous physical activity daily. It can be in the form of playing sports such as football, basketball, etc. Or it can be in the form of exercising regularly. You can go for both playing some sport and exercising. Here is how you can get a healthy amount of exercise and benefit from it.

1: Aerobic exercise

Aerobic exercises, i.e., brisk walking, jogging, swimming, cycling, etc., involve the increased inhalation of oxygen to produce energy. On the other hand, anaerobic exercises like jumping, sprinting, weightlifting, etc., take energy from the fat stored in the body instead of oxygen.

As a teenager, you should do aerobic exercise, which can keep you healthy. For example, you can go for a brisk walk once every two days. You can also choose from various aerobic exercises according to your interests. To ensure you consistently perform your aerobic exercise, you can use online tools to record your physical activities. Preferably, an app that forms streaks of your training will work best for you, as the streaks will motivate you to continue regularly.

2: Muscle-strengthening

Being intellectually smart and intelligent is very important, but being physically strong is equally significant. Your physical strength will boost your confidence and make you feel good about yourself while maintaining your health. Some of the muscle-strengthening exercises that you can perform with ease without using equipment, are the following:

- Push-ups
- Planks
- Crunches
- Jumping jacks
- Leg lifts

If you can go to the gym, you can try some safe equipment under the supervision of your parents or a fitness trainer. Whether you choose to perform muscle-strengthening exercises in your house, playground, or gym, do them at least three times a week. Add it to your schedule or to-do list. You can use some online tools to keep track of it and stay motivated to perform these exercises consistently.

3: Bone-strengthening

Bone-strengthening exercises involve weight-bearing physical activities like skipping, jumping, running, etc. These exercises can increase bone density and strengthen them. Ultimately, these exercises reduce the risk of diseases like arthritis and osteoporosis. Perform these exercises every other day (Glw & Glw, 2022).

In addition to all three types of exercises, you can play sports that combine aerobic exercise with bone-strengthening activities, such as basketball. Try to adjust your timetable and dedicate an hour each day to performing exercises and playing sports. Investing time in caring for your physical health is the best investment you can make. Exercising will play a significant part in maintaining your physical health.

What about your mental or psychological health?

Meditation can help you detach yourself from stress, anxiety, and many other issues you might be facing. It can help you see them from a better angle. In some cases, it can protect you from being negatively affected by things happening around you.

MEDITATING

Meditation is a relaxing and soothing activity involving breathing techniques to reduce stress. It enhances mindfulness and can help you focus on your studies and improve your academics. To manage stress, take a small break and reflect on your thoughts. You will learn the art of staying composed and controlling your emotions through meditation.

The best part about meditation is that it doesn't take much time. It can be done for as little as five minutes. Also, there aren't any hard-and-fast rules for meditation. It can be practiced anywhere or anytime. You can sit on the floor or a chair. As a beginner, close your eyes and don't think about anything else other than your pattern of breathing. Focus on how you take fresh air in by inhaling and exhaling particles of air. Consider the sensations you might be feeling. You can also imagine a peaceful place, like a beautiful garden or a waterfall, and explore that place in your imagination. When you are ready to open your eyes, you will notice a change in your mind and body. Embrace this change and remember the sensation. With practice, you will find that meditation can be incredibly calming and soothing.

Apart from exercising and meditating, not getting enough sleep can also be the cause of many health problems. Do you know why proper sleep is so important for your health? Let's discuss.

GETTING ENOUGH SLEEP

Sleeping well every night is vital for physical health, emotional and mental development, and academic performance (Importance of Sleep for Teenagers, 2021). While you sleep, anything you have learned, initially stored in your brain as short-term memory, turns into your long-term memory. Not getting enough sleep can disrupt the patterns of long-term memory formation (Faasm, 2022).

During sleep, the human body is controlled by the autonomic nervous system or the parasympathetic nervous system. In other words, involuntary movements, and reflexes of the body, such as breathing, etc., occur very slowly. Besides, many hormones, including the growth hormone and reproductive hormones, are produced while a person is asleep. Lack of sleep can result in the under-production of those hormones and, ultimately, their under-secretion making a person suffer from different health conditions. In short, lack of sleep can seriously threaten your health (Why Is Sleep Important? | NHLBI, NIH, 2022b).

The National Sleep Foundation and the American Academy of Sleep Medicine recommend that teens sleep between eight and ten hours a night. Quantity of sleep is just one part of the equation when it comes to good rest. The following can improve the quality of your sleep: (mindbodygreen, 2022)

- Going to bed early.
- Don't eat heavy meals before going to bed.

- Try to fall asleep within half an hour of getting into bed.
- Turn lights off.
- Don't use your phone.

CONSUMING A HEALTHY DIET

You don't need to count calories excessively or drastically remove certain foods from your diet to be healthy. Aim to follow the Mediterranean diet, which promotes good heart and mental health and helps stave off health issues like obesity and diabetes.

The Mediterranean diet comprises lean proteins, fruits and vegetables, legumes and nuts, whole grains, and healthy essential fatty acids called Omega-3s. These can be found in fish like salmon and tuna, as well as in olive oil, walnuts, and extra-virgin olive oil. This diet is also high in fiber, which helps promote a healthy gut. Your gut is populated by many bacteria that help promote good digestive health and keep depression at bay (Admin, 2022b).

Although occasional treats are fine, try to avoid consuming sweetened beverages and refined foods like cookies, pies, and fried snacks too often, as these foods can lead to obesity and health issues like Type 2 diabetes. To eat healthily without fussing too much about portions or labels, you can:

- Eat plant-based foods daily.
- Choose seasonal and fresh foods over processed ones.
- Consume healthy fats like extra-virgin olive oil or avocado oil.
- Try to grill, bake, or boil foods instead of frying them.
- Consume less red meat, as this food is high in saturated fat and can therefore increase the risk of heart disease.

The US Dietary Guidelines recommend that tweens and teens aged nine to eighteen should consume around three cups of milk/dairy products per day. Aim to have regular mealtimes, so you don't feel tempted to snack on unhealthy fast foods (Olive Tomato, 2019).

PROTECTING YOUR MENTAL HEALTH

Many teens in the US enjoy good mental health, but around 49.5% have had a mental health disorder (such as anxiety or depression) at some point in their lives. To keep your mental health in top condition, aim to:

- Exercise daily. Numerous studies have shown that exercise is a powerful stress buster. It also releases feel-good chemicals in your brain (endorphins), which put you in a great mood.
- Do something extra-special for your health every day by taking part in a specific stress-busting activity like yoga, Tai Chi, mindfulness meditation, or controlled breathing. All these methods have been found to lower stress hormone levels, improve your mood, and make you feel more motivated, focused, and energetic!
- Make time for social interaction. Feeling like part of a community or having a solid friend group can support you in tough times and provide you with mutual support for the rest of your life.
- Exercise self-compassion. This doesn't mean feeling sorry for yourself! It simply involves being as kind to yourself as you would be to someone you love. If a loved one had a problem and they were down in the dumps, would you put them down and make them feel worse? You would probably try to fix their mood, suggest spending a day together, or listen to their concerns. Be equally non-judgmental to

yourself (Self-compassion May Protect People from the Harmful Effects of Perfectionism, 2018).

Tips for Exercising Self-Compassion:

Just as we treat others with respect and try to help them through their problems, we should also be polite to ourselves (Harvard Health, 2021).

Here are some tips to practice self-compassion:

a. Say positive affirmations to yourself such as "I am a hard worker," "I am doing the best I can," "We all make mistakes sometimes," "It is tough, but I'm not going to give up," and "This can teach me something."

b. Comfort your body by asking a loved one for a massage, enjoying a relaxing walk, or eating something yummy, but healthy.

c. Write a letter to yourself about a situation that caused you pain (a lower grade than you expected at school, not being invited to someone's party), but don't blame anyone; simply describe the situation. This will help you nurture your feelings.

d. Think of what you would say to a good friend to encourage them when they are facing a difficult situation. Say the same things to yourself.

e. Spend at least 10 minutes in a natural setting every day. It can help students feel happier while lessening the effects of physical and mental stress (Spending Time in Nature Reduces Stress, Research Finds | Cornell Chronicle, 2020).

It is essential to seek help from a mental health professional if conditions like anxiety or depression are interfering with your ability to live your daily life. However, many teens are afraid to speak up, yet asking for help shows bravery and maturity, not weakness (Bulgaru, 2022). Mental health professionals can help you make big improvements through cognitive behavioral therapy, highlighting the important link between your thoughts, emotions, and behaviors. They can give you practical exercises to manage stress and tension more flexibly (Self-compassion for Pre-teens and Teenagers, 2021).

This chapter will probably keep you busy as you aim to find ways to stay fit and mentally healthy while also juggling your schoolwork and other obligations. However, you may be surprised to learn that with sound planning, you will have all the time you need to socialize, meet your obligations, and do your share of home chores. Though they may not sound like the most exciting activities on the block, once you start doing them regularly, you might be surprised to learn that you are hooked! The more skills you learn, the closer you can get to success. Continue reading to unveil another powerful skill that will lead you to success.

5

SKILL FIVE: MAKING HOME CHORES EASY AND BECOMING A SAVVY COOK

" Projects have a beginning and an end. Chores are the things you do over and over again. A"

— J. DAVID COX

Teens nowadays are pressured with studies and other activities. Consequently, they fail to recognize the importance of cooking and home chores. Around 28 percent of parents in the US cook less often with their children than they did growing up with their parents. As a result, most parents don't feel confident that their kids know how to follow a recipe (Brown-Riggs, 2017). They view them as uninteresting and unimportant. However, these activities can be fun and a source of strengthening the bond with family. Learning them can help you manage everything without stressing about it later in life.

HOW CAN DOING CHORES BENEFIT YOU?

Effective learning always starts at home. Household chores can be interesting for some people while very difficult for others. These complicated groups of tasks can help you adopt some exceptional personality traits. For example, you will have to perform these tasks regularly, even if you don't feel like doing them. As a result, you will learn consistency (7 Important Reasons Why Kids Should Have Chores, n.d.). It means you can continue doing tasks despite the complications you might face. Moreover, during this learning process, you will make mistakes and learn from them. You will accept your mistakes and work to rectify them.

Not many teens learn to manage household chores, but those who can manage these tasks effortlessly later in their lives when they become needed instead of an activity. If you start learning different home chores today, it will benefit you in the future. It doesn't mean that you start to work on everything that needs to be done at home every day. Take it one step at a time. Begin with the most straightforward task or the one that interests you the most. You can spend a small part of your day learning and managing it. Gradually, you can add more activities to your schedule. Learning these tasks is important for a successful life, so you must make time for them. It doesn't have to be long. Fifteen to thirty minutes daily can be good because the investment is worth it (Bha, 2021).

The following are some of the benefits of learning and managing household chores:

1: Teaches you skills you will use for the rest of your life

Since your childhood, you have seen your parents manage all the household chores. When you grow up and move out, you will have to manage everything by yourself. If you start doing these chores and learn how everything is done, you won't have to worry about them later in your life. You will get all the tasks done without any stress.

Most teens just don't take an interest in home chores. They have to study and want to play video games and socialize with friends. Everything they do is important and can help them learn and grow. However, not learning how to manage different tasks at home can cause them future difficulties.

Whether it is washing dishes or cleaning your room, every little task you learn to do under the supervision of your parents or by yourself will help you in the future. Yes, it's true that many appliances have made home chores easier than ever before, but learning to operate those appliances and making proper use of them is equally important (Household Chores for Children and Teenagers, 2023).

2: Boosts your confidence

Managing home chores can be an effective way of boosting your confidence. Confidence is defined as a person's belief in themselves. Learning skills can make a person capable of doing different things and ultimately strengthen their belief in themselves. Performing tasks correctly helps them trust in their abilities. And hence, it boosts their confidence.

Home chores are a bunch of powerful skills. When you perform these tasks consistently, you learn the ins and outs of every task. You become aware of the mistakes to avoid in order to perform the task in the best manner. With time and regular practice, you will hone your skills. As a result, your belief in yourself will strengthen. If someone asks you for help, you never have to say, "I am not sure how to do it." Instead, you will always be ready to help others and teach them the same skills you've learned.

3: Teaches you teamwork

Working with parents or siblings to clean the house or do laundry teaches you teamwork. In the same way you cooperate with the members of a group task at school, cooperating with family members will also make you a team player. You will learn how to work with everyone in a positive environment, teach them things you know, and help each other.

Another interesting part about working with a team is you get to experience different ways of doing one thing. For example, you can go grocery shopping with your mother for one week. And the next week, you can shop for groceries with your father. You will learn how to pick the right food for your kitchen. You can also observe how their ways are different and learn both ways. It will make you even better at doing the task.

4: Helps you understand and appreciate your parents' work

You might not be familiar with the work your parents put in to give you a neat and tidy house. You might think it doesn't take much time or effort to clean the kitchen or the living room. However, when you start doing these tasks yourself, you will realize how difficult they are. As a result, you will be able to truly appreciate your parent's work and respect it.

You will also understand how exhausted they get by the end of the day and why you should try to help your parents any time you are free during the day. Understanding them will help strengthen the bond you share.

5: Helps you build a solid work ethic

As you manage household chores, you will find it a little difficult. But if you continue doing household chores, you will get better at them. This is only possible if you follow the proper methods and do not run away from them. This will help you build a strong work ethic. So, when you enter your professional life, you won't opt for shortcuts. You will put effort into your work, no matter how difficult it is to execute and in the end you will be successful.

By working on different home chores, you will know how important it is to complete your tasks on time. You will also learn that your duty is supposed to be performed by you, and not others. This will help you become responsible in your professional life.

6: Hone your time management skills

When you start helping your parents with household chores, you will notice they are faster than you at getting things done. This is due to their years of experience and continuous practice. You can complete household chores as quickly as your parents with practice and effort. In addition, you will learn some valuable tips on how to complete multiple tasks at once from watching them.

Just think about it. There is such a long list of household chores, and most of them have to be managed every single day. It is not possible for an individual to complete daily chores without possessing exceptional time management skills. And as you clean your room and wash dishes consistently, you will learn to manage your time more effectively.

Everyone has chores they love more and those they would rather avoid. Together with your parents or guardians, you can come up with a schedule of tasks. For instance, you might prefer doing the laundry to washing the dishes (Household Chores for Adolescents, n.d.).

In general, however, you should know how to:

- Use a washing machine.
- Use a dishwasher.
- Keep your room neat and tidy.
- Help your parents in washing a car, scrubbing the bathroom, and working in the yard.
- Help with dinner.
- Walk the family dog (Lcsw, 2022b).

USING A WASHING MACHINE

Doing laundry is an exciting task if you do everything step by step. First, begin by separating white, light-colored, and dark-colored clothing. This protects white or light-colored clothes from getting stained due to color bleeding from darker clothes. Then, read the garment tags one by one. They have symbols that inform you of how the item should be washed (Mark, 2022). For instance, some clothes should not be washed above a specific temperature, while others should be dry-cleaned. You will have to be careful, as clothes can get ruined if you do not wash them as indicated.

Next, you will need to use your machine's printed or online manual to learn how to use the different cycles. These cycles will be clearly labeled, so making a choice is a matter of logic. Typical cycles include cotton, synthetics, delicates, quick wash, and hand wash (Washing Machine Cycles Explained, n.d.).

You can also choose the temperature at which the machine washes your clothes. Use the hot wash option for tough, very dirty items; warm washes for under-wear; and cold washes for lightly-to-moderately-soiled items. You can then proceed to add detergent and fabric softener in the dispenser. Add one tablespoon of detergent for a medium load. A regular or medium load means a load of clothes filling ½ of the drum. After you wash your clothes, put them inside the dryer (A Basic Guide to How to Use a Washing Machine, n.d.).

Once you have washed and dried your garments, fold them neatly and put them in your wardrobe, ironing them first if necessary.

USING A DISHWASHER

A dishwasher is just as easy to use as a washing machine. Ask your parents or an adult for help the first time you use it. They will show you where things usually go. Families place items in different spots, but some parts of the dishwasher are for specific items. For instance, many people use the upper row for glasses and bowls and the lower row for plates. There is a dedicated compartment for cutlery (Jung, 2023).

Pro tip: When using the dishwasher, place your knives facing down. Here are some more tips on using a dishwasher:

- Place the dishes in the center. While you load the lower rack of your dishwasher, make sure that all the dishes face the center. This way, the sprayer arms will easily spray water and clean the dishes properly.

- Avoid overcrowding. Overcrowding might hinder the proper supply of water and detergent to wash your dishes. Keep the dishes at some distance from one another.
- Placing items between the tines (the protrusions on the upper and lower racks).
- Don't block the sprayer arms. It's important to place items like glasses or cups in the upper rack, as they can block the sprayer arms from thoroughly spraying water on the dishes.
- Only load dishwasher-friendly items. You should not load bronze, copper, or wood in the dishwasher. These materials can be affected by the heat produced by the dishwasher (Whirlpool, 2018).

KEEPING YOUR ROOM CLEAN AND TIDY

You should keep your room tidy. It indicates how organized and responsible you are. If you can take proper care of the things you possess, you will be able to handle other responsibilities in life the right way.

Follow these steps to keep your room clean:

- Always place everything where it belongs.
- Vacuum the floors and furniture once a week. If you have a solid floor, then you may wish to sweep and mop it instead.

- Dust the items in your room every couple of days with a wet rag.
- Clean surfaces every couple of days with a surface cleaner.
- Make your bed daily, ensuring the sheets fit tightly and the bed looks symmetrical.
- See to it that the floor is completely free of paper, gadgets, clothing, and shoes.
- Keep items in the same place. Be strict about this, so you can always find what you are looking for.
- Do a deeper cleaning of your room once a month, donating, upcycling, or giving away the things you no longer need.

Helping your parents with washing a car, scrubbing the bathroom, and working in the yard.

Overall, you should try to help your parents with other chores like washing a car, scrubbing the bathroom, and working in the yard. These are a few things that do not have any hard-and-fast rules. How your parents clean the yard, trim the grass, take care of the lawn and plants, etc., are the things you might find difficult to learn on your own. Assisting your parents with these chores can help you learn these important skills easily.

Scrubbing the bathroom (sink, toilet, bathtub, and shower stall) can help protect against the transmission of different diseases. Keeping everything clean and organized is among the best skills a person can possess. So, be there with your parents while they manage household chores like these, observe their work and help them. Doing so will help you learn how to do the chores and how to do them right.

HELPING WITH DINNER

You might be responsible for cooking, doing the dishes, setting the table, or clearing the table. Talk to your parents and decide if you prefer to do the same daily task or take turns with your siblings so everyone can do different jobs.

You can help your parents in preparation for dinner. Initially, you can observe how they cook and handle cutlery and the stove. You can also learn about the use of different spices, etc. Then, you can learn to chop vegetables or make salads. Gradually, you will start cooking meals under the supervision of your parents. Before you know it, you will be cooking full-blown meals by yourself.

WALKING THE FAMILY DOG

If you love your pooch, take note: dogs need exercise to be physically and mentally healthy. Your dog should enjoy a couple of long walks a day, and you can take them for at least one of these walks. Aim to have an adult with you. If you are an older teen (aged around fourteen or fifteen) and you are used to going alone, walk your pooch in the daytime, when many people are outside.

BECOMING A CONFIDENT HOME COOK

To become a good cook, you should know how to follow a recipe, handle food safely, and understand essential cooking terms. Cooking is not rocket science. It is more of an art. It means that once you learn it, you can experiment to enhance it according to your taste. All it takes to start you on this journey is a positive mental attitude. Just believe in yourself and enjoy the mistakes you make during this journey because these mistakes will teach you things not mentioned in recipe books.

So, when you enter your kitchen, you should decide to focus on cooking and enjoy the process. After you are done making a dish, you should praise yourself. Just think of your kitchen as a scientist's lab where you have several products to experiment on. Moreover, you have a list of options to choose from. Isn't it fun? Before you enter this lab, there are some basics you should know. For example, how to follow a recipe and use different kitchen appliances and knives. etc.

How to follow a recipe?

To follow a recipe, you should identify its different parts. Some important components of a recipe are the following:

- Recipe: a set of instructions that lets you know what you are cooking.
- Servings: the proportions of ingredients according to the number of people you cook for.
- Time: the time it takes to prepare a dish.
- Ingredients: a list of ingredients you will use to make a meal.
- Directions: the order of the steps you must follow when preparing the dish.

You have learned about some important parts of a recipe. Before you start cooking, you should know how to handle food safely.

Handle the food safely

Here are some tips to handle food safely:

- Wear an apron, secure your hair, and wash your hands before preparing a dish.
- Wash the fruits and vegetables properly.
- Arrange different food types in different places to prevent cross-contamination.
- All food items have a "best before" date stamped on them. Read them before using any food item in your dish.
- Do not use your phone while cooking. It can distract you from the actual task, which can lead to accidents.

Exercising Knife Safety

It is important to handle food safely, you should learn to handle knives because it is extremely important for your safety (CrEATive Kitchen, 2017).

Follow the instructions mentioned below to ensure your safety while using a knife:

- Fix the cutting board in its place so it doesn't slip when you are cutting something. For this, you can use a wet piece of cloth and place it under the cutting board; it will create friction and prevent the board from moving.

- Always cut the round vegetables in half along their length before you start chopping them. It will prevent them from rolling.
- Use a sharp knife while cutting because dull knives will make you exert more pressure while cutting, and you can accidentally hurt yourself.
- It is advisable to use your knife while standing.
- Use different knives for cutting vegetables and meat to prevent contamination.

Cooking terms to master

Familiarizing yourself with some basic cooking terminology can make it easy to follow a recipe (Lowry, n.d.).

The following are the most used cooking terms:

- Slice: To cut something along the grain uniformly.
- Roast: Exposing the food to heat for a good amount of time by placing it in the oven or over the fire.
- Chop: Cutting the food into bite-sized pieces.
- Fry: Cooking in oil.
- Grate: To rub food with a grater to divide it into small shreds.

- Knead: Working the dough with your hands.
- Season: To add salt and spices to food.
- Steam: To cook something with the steam of boiling water.
- Beat: To stir a mixture thoroughly.
- Dice: Cutting food into fine cubes.
- Saute: To fry something quickly in hot oil.
- Stir-fry: Frying food while stirring it.
- Whisk: Beating and stirring a mixture.
- Dredge: Coating food with dry powder or flour.
- Peel: To remove the skin of a fruit or vegetable.
- Crush: To reduce food to crumbs by exerting weight on it.
- Pour: Adding a liquid steadily into a container.

THREE RECIPES TO COOK

Do you feel intimidated by cooking or think you can't arrange a dinner party for friends?

You can do it without worrying about what to cook or how. Here are three dishes you can prepare for your dinner party and amaze everyone with your cooking skills. You will learn to cook a starter, main, and dessert dish. And do you know the best part? These dishes are highly low-key and won't require much time to make. Excited to learn? Let's get started.

A Starter: Blini Pancakes

The preparation time for blini pancakes is around 5 minutes, and the cooking time is 15 minutes. You can prepare this dish in less than 30 minutes.

Ingredients that you need are:

- Organic Buckwheat Flour - 75g
- Baking powder - 1 tsp
- Pinch of salt
- Egg - 1
- Milk - 150 ml
- Oil for frying

You can make 40 to 45 small blini pancakes by using these ingredients, which make approximately 8 servings. You can increase or decrease the proportions of ingredients according to the servings you want.

Utensils that you will need for preparing blini pancakes:

- Large Frying pan
- Mixing bowls - x 2

Directions for preparation:

- Add the dry ingredients, i.e., flour, baking powder, and salt in a bowl and mix well.
- Sieve the ingredients into a mixing bowl.
- Add half the milk to this mixture and one egg. Then, beat this mixture into a smooth paste.
- Pour the remaining milk and beat.
- Your batter is ready.
- Take a large frying pan and add 2 tablespoons of oil. Move the oil in a circular motion to adequately cover the pan's surface, and heat until the pan is nice and hot.
- Use a teaspoon to drop the batter onto the pan to make small blini pancakes.

- When one side of the pancakes turns golden with small bubbles on it, flip them to cook the other side as well.
- Transfer the cooked blinis to a cooling rack.
- Repeat with the remaining batter.
- Add the toppings of your choice, serve, and enjoy (Netmums, 2022).

An Entrée Dish: Crispy Chicken Parmesan

The preparation time for crispy chicken parmesan is 10 minutes, while it can take around 40 minutes to cook. The proportions mentioned in the ingredients below will be enough for four servings. You can start by roasting the chicken breasts coated with the egg mixture and bread-crumbs. In the meantime, you can prepare the sauce. Once the chicken is roasted, you can top it with parmesan cheese, and finally, you can serve it with spaghetti or salad.

Ingredients:

For the chicken:

- Chicken breasts - 2
- Egg - 1
- Breadcrumbs - 50g
- Oil - 1 tbsp
- Smoked paprika - 0.5 tsp
- salt and pepper

For the sauce:

- Oil - 1 tsp
- Diced onion - 1
- Crushed garlic cloves - 2
- Chopped tomatoes - 1
- Balsamic vinegar - 1 tbsp
- Dried basil - 0.5 tsp

To top:

- Grated mozzarella - 40g

- Grated parmesan - 20g

To serve:

- Cooked spaghetti for kids
- Salad/veggies for adults

You need:

- An oven
- A knife for cutting chicken and another knife for vegetables
- Bowl 2
- Whisk
- Saucepan

Directions:

- Preheat the oven to 400°F.
- Slice each chicken breast into two halves lengthwise.
- Break the egg and add it to a bowl. Whisk it to get a consistent mixture.
- Take another bowl and add breadcrumbs, oil, and smoked paprika to it. Season with a little salt and pepper. Mix it well.

- Take the chicken breasts and dip them one by one into the egg, then coat them in the mixture of breadcrumbs.
- Place the coated chicken breasts on a tray and bake in the oven for 25 minutes.
- In the meantime, take a saucepan, add oil, diced onions, and crushed garlic to it.
- Fry for 2-3 minutes.
- Add the chopped tomatoes, balsamic vinegar, and dried basil to the saucepan.
- Bring to a boil, and then simmer for 15 minutes.
- Once the chicken is roasted, remove the tray.
- Add a few spoonfuls of the sauce to the top of each chicken breast and top it with grated mozzarella and grated parmesan.
- Transfer the chicken to the oven for another 10 minutes.
- Serve the dish with salad/veggies or spaghetti depending on your taste (Attwell, 2021).

A Dessert: Fruity Skewers With Yogurt Dip

The prep time for fruity skewers is 20 minutes. You don't need to cook it. The proportions of ingredients mentioned below will be enough for four servings.

Ingredients:

- Bananas – 2
- Grapes - 1 cup
- Strawberries - 1 cup
- Blueberries - ½ cup
- Yogurt - 1 cup
- Maple syrup – 1 tbsp
- Cinnamon - (for sprinkling)

You will need:

- Knife
- Cutting board
- Skewers
- Bowl
- Teaspoon

Directions:

- Take a cutting board and place it on the working surface.
- Peel the skin of the banana and place it on the cutting board.
- Cut it into small slices.
- You can transfer the sliced bananas to a separate plate.
- Cut the strawberries into halves.
- Place the fruits onto the skewers.
- Add maple syrup to yogurt and sprinkle cinnamon on it (Best, 2022).

All these dishes are easy to prepare and take relatively little time. All you have to do is handle the food safely. You will enjoy preparing these dishes, for sure!

Now that you know how to keep your home clean, do your laundry, and cook a few dishes, you probably feel more confident about leaving home and going to college.

In the next chapter, I will highlight key strategies for planning for college and finding a job. Teens dream of ideal professional lives, but not everyone succeeds in turning these dreams into reality.

What can help you get into college and achieve your dream job?

6

SKILL SIX: PLAN FOR COLLEGE AND WORK

"Work while they sleep, learn while they party, save while they spend. Live like they dream."

— *ANONYMOUS*

A 2021 survey found that over 80 percent of college students wish they had learned more life skills before going to college. Many are completely lost when it comes to investing money, planning long-term financial goals, and managing their student loans. College students have also expressed worry about being unable to do laundry, cook healthy meals, or do simple things like reset Wi-Fi routers.

The decisions you make when you are a teen can make or break your plans for years to come. Therefore, considerations like planning your finances, selecting the right college, and trying to earn a little income are vital in your last few years of high school.

CHOOSING THE RIGHT COLLEGE

Choosing the right college isn't easy. Some individuals choose one based on their personal preferences. For example, if they have been following the social media site of a specific college and are blown away by its beautiful buildings and infrastructure, they might choose it.

Do you think it's a good idea to choose a college because its visual appearance attracted you?

There is nothing wrong with this method, some important factors must be considered before choosing a college. Because the purpose of selecting a college is to seek education so that you gain enough knowledge and skills to live a successful professional life. Therefore, you need to make this decision carefully. Look at some factors to keep in mind while you opt for a college:

1: College rankings

College rankings are important when selecting a college since a top ranking in your field will increase your likelihood of obtaining employment in your chosen field. The standard of education and the presence of the best academic staff can make some colleges stand out from the rest. All these things create a learning environment that can benefit you in the best way.

Another advantage that you can get by choosing a high-ranked college is the company of highly accomplished intellectuals. So, the opportunities to learn will increase. Having said that, rankings aren't the only factor to consider before choosing a college. As there are many things that should be taken into consideration: time, the distance of your college from where you live, tuition fee, course duration, ease of changing majors, etc. (Reneau, 2021)

2: Distance from where you live and transport costs

When selecting a college, you must consider the distance of different colleges from your home before choosing one. The location of a college is important because it can play a significant role in shaping your college experience. For example, if your commute to the college is more than 30 minutes, you might feel tired and unfocused when you arrive, making it difficult to concentrate on your studies. You could also feel exhausted at the end of the day and lack the energy to study or perform extracurricular activities. It can affect your overall performance in college as well. If you don't use this travel time for something productive, like listening to an audiobook or working on an assignment, it can be a waste of time.

Some people suffer from motion sickness while traveling and can't get over it quickly. Therefore, their entire day is affected by this issue. Moreover, transport costs can add to your college expenses, increasing your responsibilities. This can negatively impact your academic performance and overall college experience.

3: How expensive is tuition?

Depending on how you are planning to pay for your tuition fees, you should consider the tuition of different colleges. Some students' parents can pay the college tuition, while others must work part-time jobs and apply for student funds or scholarships. It can often be stressful if you select a college with costly and unaffordable tuition. But you don't have to burden yourself by choosing an overly expensive college. It doesn't mean you have to compromise the standard of education. Many colleges offer excellent courses with relatively affordable tuition. Do thorough research to find the right college for you.

4: How long is your course?

Course duration is important because it can give you a general idea of the depth of information you are going to cover in that course. It is also important to predict your graduation time, as you might be looking forward to your professional life. Longer course durations can hinder you from starting your full-time job or any business early, when you have the potential to do your best. See if the course duration suits your goals, needs, and schedule.

5: *The social, cultural, and mental health offerings of your shortlisted colleges.*

Apart from studies, understanding social and cultural diversity among different parts of the world is very important. It can help form your entire view of the world and understand different people. So, a college that conducts different social and cultural awareness events now and then can be very important.

Additionally, the mental health offerings of a college should be considered. The availability of counselors and health professionals and access to them is a bonus. Students face stressful situations in college and there should always be someone to reach out to for help.

6: *The ease of changing majors*

Sometimes students find their chosen course uninteresting or difficult, and therefore they want to change it. Many universities offer the service of changing your major, but the procedure can be draining and exhausting. As a result, many students prefer to drop out. So, you need to be mentally prepared. Do the research to know about the ease of changing majors at your shortlisted universities and prioritize the ones where you can easily change your major. Because changing a major you aren't interested in is better than studying it for years or dropping out of college (Top 10 Factors for Choosing a College, n.d.).

After you have selected a college, you will need finances for your tuition. You can work part-time and take out student loans. You must calculate whether your starting salary will be enough for your student loan. Use a loan calculator like Calculator Soup for this purpose. Bear in mind that your monthly payment should not be more than the eight percent gross salary limit. The US Department of Education recommends not borrowing over eight percent of your gross project income or twenty percent of your discretionary income. Your discretionary income is the amount you retain after deducting taxes, social security charges, and basic living costs (Nickolas, 2022).

TAKING OUT A SUITABLE STUDENT LOAN

a. If you need to take out a student loan, aim to borrow no more than 8 percent of your projected gross income, as recommended by the US Department of Education (Nesbit, 2022). This should be done to pay back the loan without any difficulty. If you exceed this percentage, you might create serious problems for yourself, as managing finances with little income will become difficult (Lane & Branch, 2023).

b. Work out how much you need to borrow by including all your expenses, including housing, food, clothing, and entertainment costs. Subtract any grants, amounts provided by your family, and scholarships from the total amount.

c. Fill out the Free Application for Federal Student Aid (FAFSA). This form helps college students to receive grants, loans, scholarships, and work-study programs from the United States Government. Be careful while filling in information. Do not make any mistakes or provide false information.

d. Research the different types of federal loans you may qualify for. It is important to help you find the best loans for you with easy payment policies.

e. Research private loan options but remember they may not have as many repayment plan options as federal loans. Private loans may also have a fixed or variable rate. In general, it is advisable to opt for a fixed loan because variable rates can change monthly or quarterly and give you a surprise (Lockert, 2022).

f. When comparing different loans, look at factors such as the repayment term, interest rate, monthly payment, and different repayment options (Helhoski, 2022).

As you start your college life, you can choose to live in a dorm or find an apartment. Here are some tips to help you find the right apartment.

FINDING THE RIGHT ACCOMMODATION

Boarding at college may be a good idea for your first year, as it will enable you to get used to your campus and its surroundings. However, you may eventually wish to share an apartment with other students to lower your cost (Collegiate Parent, 2021). If so, keep the following tips in mind:

- Choose trustworthy roommates who make similar lifestyle choices to your own. One of the problems college students faces is uncooperative roommates. If you are suffering from homesickness and your roommates aren't supportive, your psychological health can be affected. Moreover, you won't be able to focus on your studies or your work.
- Find out about the lease before you sign it. Work out who is responsible for repairing broken equipment, whether parking is available, the length of the lease, what utilities and appliances are available. This can help you

calculate the expenses in advance and see if the apartment is affordable or not.

- Conduct research online and talk to other students regarding the best places to live and nearby transportation options. Some online tools can help you locate apartments near your college that are free to rent. You can contact the apartment owner, then, and ask for the details (7 Tips to Finding the Perfect College Apartment | Central Bank, n.d.).

Having a part-time job is an essential part of college life, not only because you have to pay tuition but also to become financially stable and enjoy your student life. You don't necessarily have to go for a job requiring a lot of time and energy. Try to find convenient jobs that are close to both your college and your apartment. This way, you will reach your workplace on time and won't be spending much on transportation.

HAVING A PART-TIME JOB WHILE STUDYING

Around 40% of full-time and 74% of part-time students work while studying (COE - College Student Employment, n.d.). There are many benefits to working while you learn. You can manage your expenses independently and gain experience while completing your degree. As a result, by the time you graduate, you will be a learned and experienced professional. You can, then, search for a better job for yourself or build a startup.

Here are a few examples of part-time jobs college students choose while studying include:

- Online content writer: Many online platforms require a content writer to write articles and blogs. As a college student, it can be a convenient method of earning money and will help you learn a lot. The job will require you to research different topics and write about them.
- Barista: Working as a barista can be fun and can teach you different skills such as customer handling, time management, etc. As a barista, you will be responsible for preparing coffee, decorating it, and serving it.
- Tutor: Another job that most college students go for is tutoring. If you are good at a skill, you can instruct others.
- Teacher: Teaching can also be a convenient job for you as a college student. It is very beneficial for enhancing your knowledge, as teaching is one of the best methods of learning.
- Waiter: Another simple but beneficial job is that of a waiter. It teaches you many things about

customer behavior and customer handling, which can help later in your professional life.

- Babysitter: If you are someone who can take care of children properly, you can become a babysitter. This role will require you to care for a child when their parents are away.

- Translator: If you know more than one language, you can become a translator. Much of online content is being translated into different languages, so you can use this as an opportunity to work.

- Receptionist: It is a simple job that can help you learn about customer care, how to communicate effectively, and interact with clients.

- Cashier: Cash handling for a small business can be an option for you. You will have to work responsibly, though. It might require you to be good with numbers.

Tips for Finding a Job

Financial independence is among the most satisfying and beneficial things in an individual's life. Being able to manage their expenses by themselves is every teen's dream. They look forward to it and wait for the moment in their lives when they will finally start working.

Teens have many expectations regarding their professional lives and their dream jobs. However, life can be harsh sometimes. Things might not turn out the way you expect. So, you should be prepared to cope with any unexpected situations in life. Becoming financially stable after moving out can be difficult, but if you start preparing for it today, you won't have to worry about it in the future. This preparation involves gathering the skills, personality traits, and knowledge for your job. Make a list of all the skills that you need to master to become an ideal candidate for the job you would like to choose in the future. What traits should you adopt to become the best at your job? Where can you acquire the knowledge, you need to perform your job? Find the answers to all these questions and start working on yourself. For example, if Chloe wants to become a software engineer, she needs to learn and work on different programming languages. Then, she should enroll in the software engineering program at a college to gain advanced knowledge of software engineering.

Furthermore, you should prepare yourself mentally for alternative jobs. It doesn't mean you don't believe in your abilities. It simply means that you are leaving room for possibilities. You are adopting a flexible plan for your future goals. This way, you will always have your backup plan if anything goes wrong due to any reason. For example, the market might get saturated, and you can't find the job you have been hoping for.

Some students take a gap year after high school. Others choose to go to college and graduate. Whether you want to take a gap year or go to college, a full-time or part-time job can be very helpful for your financial future. Even if your part-time job has nothing to do with your future goals, it can still teach you professionalism and work ethics. And both will help you grow in your professional life.

How can you find the right job and get it? Here are some steps you can follow to find a job for yourself, start managing your expenses, and contribute to paying tuition for your college:

1: Using the community or college resources available to you

Different colleges have given their students opportunities to work while they study. For this purpose, colleges have a career services office to guide their students and help them find a job. If your college has its own recruitment resources, you can learn more about them and try to search for a job (Hopsicker, 2022).

Usually, events such as seminars, job fairs, and meetings are organized for public awareness and assistance in finding jobs. You should look for events like these, as attending them can help you in different ways. It can help you socialize and connect with like-minded people, give you awareness of how you can achieve your goals, and motivate you to achieve your dreams.

2: Putting together a professional-looking resume.

While you search for a job, attend community sessions, and stay in touch with the recruitment services of your college, don't forget to formulate a professional-looking resume. A resume is a brief description of who you are, what skills you possess, and how your skills can benefit the company you are applying for. Just like a sales pitch is successful when it is delivered the right way and has the potential to provide the solution to the audience's problems, a resume speaks of how your abilities can solve the problems of the employer or how you are the right fit for the gap they want to fill.

Let's say you are applying for the position of tutor. Before you formulate a resume, ask yourself why a tutor is needed. Write down all the reasons that come to your mind. Then, mark off all the requirements that you can fulfill as a tutor. When you create your resume, mention all these problems to your potential employer that you are qualified to address. It will leave a positive impression on them. In addition, you should reveal that you are open to feedback and are committed to growing personally and professionally. Your resume will make them believe you understand and can perform the job best.

Follow the instructions mentioned below to create a good résumé:

- Your resume should not exceed two pages.
- Add a summary, including, qualifications, and experience (if any).
- Add soft skills such as communication skills, the ability to work in a team, etc.
- Mention the hard skills related to the job you are applying for.
- You can mention your hobbies if you want. This can help them identify if you spend your time in some productive activities or not.
- Write a brief paragraph addressing the question: "What makes you the best candidate for this position?"

3: Harnessing the power of social media

Social media has become a powerful tool to use for different purposes. Many people run online businesses by opening online stores on social media. There are different sites that can help connect like-minded people. You can also join these sites and communicate with a diverse set of people. You might not find a job opportunity right away, but you will learn from the experiences of the people you communicate with. They might have been a part of the job market longer, and they might be able to guide you regarding the dos and don'ts of your job.

You can also join social media groups that post jobs on a daily, weekly, or monthly basis. This way, you will get notified about any vacancies, so you can apply in a timely manner. There are two types of jobs you can get this way: online jobs and on-site jobs.

Online jobs can be performed from any part of the world with a stable Wi-Fi connection and required electronic devices. However, on-site jobs will require you to commute to your workplace. If you get an on-site job, check if your schedule can accommodate it. Moreover, you might need to find a job that is at a convenient distance from your place, so it doesn't create any problems.

4: Networking, both online and in person

Networking is an extremely important part of professional life. It is because opportunities won't knock at your door on their own. You will have to create a bridge toward opportunities. It can only happen when you stay in touch with people working in the industry you are interested in. It can be done through online platforms or by attending seminars and events where you can interact with different people. Communicating with these individuals, getting to know them, and letting them know you can play an important role in paving the way toward different opportunities.

How you communicate your thoughts and behave in a gathering tells a lot about you. It can depict how responsible you can be in handling a task you are trusted with.

Let's say Daisy (a college student) meets Edgar (a recruitment manager) at a formal gathering. If she listens to him carefully and interacts with Edgar in a way to learn from him, she can leave a good impression. On the other hand, if she overshares a list of things, she is good at, Edgar might think she is desperate for a job. The impression she can leave, therefore, can be negative.

5: *Aim to develop relationships with HR personnel or people who are hiring rather than sending an impersonal letter*

As explained previously, building healthy and positive relationships with experienced professionals is the key to success. All it takes is confidence and a positive attitude. Learning is far more important than finding a job. Yes, it's true that you might be eager to start managing your expenses but take things slow. The better foundation you establish for your professional life, the more beneficial it will become for you.

So, as you start networking and socializing, do it with the mindset of learning from professionals, acknowledging their hard work, and celebrating their success. If HR personnel or other professionals you socialize with find the potential in you, they will provide you with opportunities (Doyle, 2021).

Preparing for your first interview

The first interview is always special, but equally stressful. You can feel nervous, excited, confused, or anxious before your interview. It's natural to feel all these emotions, but you should prepare yourself mentally for both situations, i.e., passing the interview or failing it.

It will require a positive mindset and confident body language. Prepare for the answers the interviewer may ask. Most questions are about the key skills mentioned in the job description. Sometimes the interviewer analyzes your ability to work under pressure and whether or not you can deal with stressful situations.

Prepare well for questions like:

-How can you prove you have the knowledge and skills required for this position?

-What have you done in the past that demonstrates the best usage of your skill set?

Finally, be honest and truthful. While you describe your abilities, be straightforward. Do not lie, as it can cause many problems for you. Do not exaggerate the truth while creating your CV (Curriculum Vitae) either. Be honest and concise. It builds trust between you and the employer and can benefit you a lot in the long run.

If you pass the interview, you will have a new responsibility in your life. You will be providing your services to a business. It will require hard work and dedication to help the business grow. On the other hand, if you fail, you will learn from your mistakes and will avoid repeating them in the future.

In this chapter, you learned how to choose a college, understand student loans, and received tips on how to find a part-time job while you are studying, or a full-time job if you forgo or postpone college.

By the time you are in college, you may already be earning a salary and working out how to live on it. The next chapter will focus on helping you budget, save, and invest your money.

7

SKILL SEVEN: SAVING AND MAKING MONEY

"The key to money is to stay invested."

— *SUZE ORMAN*

D o you know that around 83% of teens do not know how to manage money? (Tuggle, 2016)

This can be problematic because, when you start managing your finances, you adopt different ways of spending. These ways eventually become your financial habits, which means that wise preferences and spending patterns can lead to better spending habits.

However, if an individual doesn't know how to spend their money and where to spend it, they can adopt poor spending habits. Nonetheless, these habits eventually determine your financial future. Modifying these habits can bring immense changes.

According to a recent report, the average student debt in the US is $32,731. However, despite this fact, it has almost become a necessity due to increased expenses. But you should never forget that the key to dealing with debt successfully is eliminating it quickly. Otherwise, debts can interfere with your ability to buy a car or a home or embark on a business project that can take your finances to the next level.

You can eliminate your debts using some powerful budgeting techniques. Let's learn about them in detail.

CREATING (AND STICKING TO) A BUDGET

Just like you create a schedule to manage your time effectively, creating a budget can be highly beneficial for managing money and repaying your student debt on time. Following are some tips to help you create a budget:

- Identify the difference between needs and wants. You can make a list of things you spend your money on. Then, write against each of them whether it's something you need or want.

- Use an Excel sheet or book to write down all your monthly expenses and how much you earn. This will help you organize everything and evaluate your income and expenditures.
- Aim to make monthly savings. Saving money gives you a sense of security. You can spend without having to worry about going bankrupt. For this purpose, have at least three times your monthly expenses saved in your bank account. It is also important for tackling future emergencies or unexpected expenses.
- Consider following the 50/30/20 rule, which is a standard method of making a budget. It stipulates that 50 percent of your income should go towards fixed needs (like your housing and supermarket costs), and 30 percent should go towards variable expenses (think clothes shopping or buying computer games). And 20 percent should be saved (Doulis, 2022).
- Note that for larger loans (such as student loans), some financial experts recommend using the 60/20/20 rule. It states that 60 percent of your income should go towards living expenses, 20 percent should go towards debt reduction, emergency funds, and

investments, and 20 percent should go towards discretionary spending (like shopping, dining out, etc.) (Doulis, 2022).

- If you receive extra cash as a gift or bonus, set aside a little more than you usually do, but feel free to enjoy the gift as well.

- Use budgeting apps like Mint, YNAB, or Goodbudget to work out how you can save more. These apps show everything you have spent your earnings on. Try to identify potential money-wasters that could be stopping you from sticking to your budget (N, 2022).

STRATEGIES FOR TEEN INVESTORS

While others work for a salary, you can invest your money and make a passive income. Investing your money can sometimes be risky, but there is nothing wrong with taking calculated risks. On the other hand, if you save your money and do not invest it, you might be unable to turn your bigger dreams into reality. Money can enhance the quality of your life. It can provide you with better facilities. If you learn the strategies of investing, it can help you know how to make money. So, without further ado, let's dive in.

Making your first forays into investment

You need to be an adult to buy stocks or shares in a company, but you can invest if a parent or trusted guardian is willing to help. Before you start investing, you should learn about the terms mentioned below.

- *Assets*: Anything that holds monetary value is called an asset.
- *Stocks*: Stock is the equity, or the share of possession, of a business.
- *Bonds*: It's a document ensuring the security of a debt you lend to an organization.
- *Diversification*: A strategy used to invest in different assets instead of any one asset to reduce the risks.

- *Risk*: It is the possibility of enduring loss in an investment.
- *Mutual funds*: Professionally managed investments made by more than one person or organization.
- *Exchange-traded funds*: A group of assets that allow investors to buy or sell shares.
- *Index funds:* An investment where you can track the financial success and failure of different businesses in the market (Bruce, 2022).
- *Interest*: Extra amount charged by the lender to the borrower.
- *Compound interest*: Interest gained from interest is called compound interest.
- *Dollar-cost averaging*: Investing over a period of time.
- *Net worth*: Total value of an asset is its net worth.
- *Custodial investment account*: Financial accounts for children that are managed by their parents or guardians (Woods, 2015).

Making an investment

Now that you are familiar with some basic terms related to investments, let's proceed to the next step, which is making the investment.

Once you decide to invest and have gained basic stock knowledge, you must research and learn how everything works. You should also learn to analyze the stock market, which will help you make informed decisions and take calculated risks. Next, you should identify investments that are appropriate for people your age. Exchange-Traded Funds (ETFs) are often recommended to new investors because they are low-cost and hold a basket of stocks or other securities from a diversified group of companies that trade (7 Steps to Investing as a Teenager [in 2023] - TeenVestor, n.d.).

Beware of investment scams! Do your research before investing, and only invest in trusted companies. Many investment schemes are scams, such as different pyramid schemes that require you to bring in more investors. Moreover, if an organization claims to give you high returns on investment in very little time, be aware and gather more information about them before investing.

If you are considering investing in a company, it is essential to check its annual reports. You can enlist the help of your parents or guardian to understand the company's financial state. Doing this would reduce the risk of investing by looking at the company's financial data, like the debt and price-to-earnings ratios.

Investing can be a relatively safer option if the company is growing financially.

As a beginner, a mock portfolio is the best tool to start investing in. You can experiment with your mock portfolio without fear of losing your money. It is a simulation of the original stock market. You can invest in stocks, bonds, or funds, and their activity in the original market will give you an idea of how good or bad your decisions were. This way, you will learn about investments in a controlled environment.

Another vital aspect of making money through investment is opening the right type of account. It is recommended to discuss the different options with parents, trusted adults, or an adult who specializes in investment and finance (Adams, 2023).

You can choose from various account types, including:

- A jointly owned brokerage account or a custodial account with your parent or guardian. A joint brokerage account is shared by two or more individuals. A custodial account, meanwhile, is a savings account set up and managed by an adult for a minor.
- A simple brokerage account is specifically set up for kids. With this type of account, you won't need your parents to act as the custodian.

The ownership of the account is yours. However, it is still wise to ask your parents to monitor your activity. With this account, you can buy stocks, bonds, mutual funds, and ETFs for many different investment options.

- If you are earning an income, you can have a Roth IRA in your own name. This account will allow you to invest tax-free for your retirement. Roth IRAs are ideal for children, as the little investments over time can pay them back heavily (O'Shea & Taube, 2023).

- Investing in index funds in an Acorns Early account can help you have a high-yield savings account. It allows you to dabble in various types of assets (including stocks, bonds, and commodities like gold). Acorns Early is considered one of the top investing apps for kids and young adults.

You have read about some investment strategies and gained basic knowledge about different financial accounts. Now it's time to move to the next step, which is starting a business. Everyone has a unique skill or talent that they can use to start a business.

If owning a business interest you, why not turn this dream into reality?

STARTING A BUSINESS

Starting a business is a great way to get ahead of debt or avoid it altogether. It can also provide you with financial education and finance management. Moreover, a business of your own can help you reach new heights in your financial success. It requires effort, hard work, and more time than a job might take, but the output it garners may be exceptional as well. To become a teen entrepreneur, you might want to consider the following:

- Start small, with a business you already have knowledge and experience in. For instance, you might start a babysitting or dog-sitting business, tutor younger kids, sell merchandise online, record unboxings and reviews for your YouTube channel, design websites, or create written content (Aebischer, 2023).

- Make sure your business allows you to work flexible hours, so you can work longer hours during your free time and work shorter hours during exam time and other key responsibilities in your life.
- Ensure your business requires a small financial investment, and before you embark on it, make a simple business plan (Revolution, 2022).
- When making your plan, research your competitors, write down the products they are selling, the price of their products, the gap you think you can fill, and the way you plan on filling that gap.
- Pitch your product to potential investors. If you need money to get your business going, pitch your potential plan to your parents or trusted adults with an interest in teen entrepreneurship.
- Learn the 4 Ps of marketing. These enable you to make your product or service attractive to potential customers and investors.
- Product: The product you have chosen to sell should have a demand in the market. You

should also try to make its quality better than other such products available on the market.

- Price: The pricing of the product determines the margin. This means that if you have manufactured a light bulb for $10 and sold it for $15, you are making a profit of $5.
- Promotion: It involves the publicity of the product. How you make your potential audience aware of the availability of your product is very important to generate sales.
- Place: If you are setting up a store, customers can visit and buy the products. However, if you are selling your products online, hiring a trusted logistics company can be helpful in distributing your products among customers.

Are you making a profit?

Once your business is up and running, subtract your expenses from the total income received to work out if the business is profitable or not.

In this chapter, you have learned about investing and becoming a shareholder of a company. You have also learned a few tips to start your small business successfully and pay off student loans. Moreover, you learned about the importance of budgeting and saving money. If you manage your money wisely, you will never have to worry about your expenses ever again. Always remember that money has the power to attract more money. So instead of keeping it in your bank account, you can invest it in stocks or start your own business.

Now that you know how to cook, tidy up, protect your health, and even start a business, the next step involves keeping yourself safe so you can enjoy all your hard work!

8

SKILL EIGHT: STAYING SAFE ONLINE AND IN EVERYDAY LIFE

"Safety is not an option; it is a requirement."

— UNKNOWN

As you enter adulthood, you may move away from your family home and live independently for the first time in your life. This might be the case if you go to college in another state or get a job that requires you to move away from home.

As a child, it is easy to take safety for granted since parents are usually in charge. When you're on your own, however, you need to look after your safety in a more productive and mindful manner. Statistics have shown that over one million burglaries occur in the US every year (Biermeier, 2022).

Another shocking stat reveals that women who live alone have a higher risk of experiencing crime than men. For all these reasons, you must take appropriate measures for your safety, and you should know how to make it out of an emergency cautiously.

STAYING SAFE AT HOME AND IN YOUR NEIGHBORHOOD

If you want to ensure your safety and avoid any unforeseen and unfortunate events, start taking steps today. Make it a habit to implement daily safety practices such as locking all windows and doors, turning the lights on outdoors when it gets dark, and avoiding night walks when you are alone.

Some people do not take safety seriously because they have never experienced crime. For Example, someone might leave their keys inside the vehicle after parking, assuming it won't get stolen. However, this increases the risk of theft. By being careless, they are putting their property in danger.

It is important to remember that just because something has never happened before doesn't mean it cannot occur in the future. You can protect yourself by taking safety precautions. Along with basic safety measures such as installing motion sensor lights outsides. These lights automatically turn on after detecting motion. This means that the lights will turn on if a burglar tries to break in through the windows or the door. The lights will startle the burglar and make you aware of the presence of someone outside your house. If something like that happens, do not panic because numerous things can also cause motion sensor lights to flicker or turn on. It can be your pet or a stray animal. So, before you dial a number for immediate help, confirm if there's someone out there. You can also install a security system with cameras that cover all areas outside and inside your home, except for select spaces.

You should also use smart technology such as video doorbells, water leak detectors, and smart thermostats. Because the dangers don't necessarily occur only outside the house. You can also face different problems inside the house. So, you should keep your house well-equipped to identify and solve a problem quickly.

Another important thing you can do to ensure your safety is to make friends in your neighborhood. Exchange phone numbers with them and agree to help each other out. Your neighbors are the closest to your house. If you need help, they can reach out to you before anyone else. Being on good terms with them can prove beneficial for both of you. Additionally, you can create a list of emergency numbers. Take a journal and write down different emergency contact numbers on it. You can list the nearest hospital, fire department, water and power company, locksmith, local emergency medical services, police department, etc. (Edwards, 2022)

To keep your house and belongings protected, don't announce your vacations on social media. By doing so, no one will know that you are not in your house, which will reduce the risk of burglary. You can post pictures and information about the vacations once you return home. Moreover, have someone with you when repairpersons are in your home, as it is unsafe to be alone when strangers are in your house. You can ask for help from your neighbors or call a friend. Also, do not bring strangers to your home, especially at night (15 Safety Tips for Living Alone - Hippo, n.d.).

STAYING SAFE WHEN YOU GO OUT AT NIGHT

Serious crimes are more commonplace at night. This doesn't mean that you should stop going out at night. All you need to do is take some basic safety measures to protect yourself. Always remember to refuse alcohol when you are out at night, as it can make you unaware of your surroundings and make you an easy target for criminals. Similarly, refuse to get into a car with a driver who has been drinking. Because they might not be in their senses while driving, which can lead to an accident. Moreover, book your ride before you leave home. This way, you won't have to wait for a taxi in the street. Even if you have to walk down a street, avoid being in poorly lit areas and keep your valuables hidden from plain sight (Spunout, 2020).

If you are attending a late-night party, stay close to your group of friends and do not separate from them or leave a club alone. You should also try to drink in moderation. Never leave your drink unattended. Sometimes, in social settings, people get into arguments, and the situation becomes aggressive. You should try to stay away from all such situations.

STAYING SAFE ONLINE

Did you know that 64.4% of the world's population uses the Internet? (Internet and Social Media Users in the World 2023 | Statista, 2023) This means that businesses can now be managed online through e-banking or e-commerce. Although personal and professional information is shared over the internet, it's generally safe to do so. However, some loopholes on the internet have enabled hackers and phishers to steal the personal data of internet users. Online assets and money can also be stolen if their security isn't strong enough. In

2022, it caused an estimated 6 trillion worth of damage. Cybercrime is on the rise. However, the financial damage is just the tip of the iceberg regarding online safety (Vojinovic & Vojinovic, 2023).

Cyberbullying is another major problem, affecting around 37% of people aged 12 to 17 (11 Facts About Cyberbullying, n.d.). Teens are more likely to become targets of cybercriminals because they can easily be convinced, can't protect themselves, and cannot raise their voices against criminals or bring them to trial. Not just cybercriminals, but random internet users can bully others too. If someone gets access to your personal information, they can threaten you with disclosing it online. This is a form of cyberbullying.

So, how can you protect yourself against all forms of cyberbullying?

Strategies for Protecting Yourself Online

Staying safe online involves keeping things private. Remember that anything you upload can be shared with a myriad of people in a matter of seconds. So, if there is some important information that you don't want to share with the online community, keep it private. Moreover, you should respect others' privacy too. Try not to share someone's personal information with others. Also, avoid sharing someone's messages without their permission, and make sure to ask for consent before recording someone's audio or video. Because when you keep others' information safe, they will probably do the same for you (How to Help Teenagers Stay Safe Online | British Council, n.d.).

Aim to be polite when interacting with others online. Treating people with respect and kindness makes you more likely to receive the same treatment in return. However, you don't have to be too friendly with strangers because you don't know their intentions. By being friendly, you will depict yourself as an easy target. It doesn't mean you should misbehave with them; rather, you should ignore them or block them. You can also enhance the security or privacy of your social media accounts so that only your friends and people you know can contact you.

Furthermore, avoid sharing private photos or information online. Because once you upload something on the internet, removing it becomes very difficult. Cybercriminals can bully or harass you. It can also lead to concerns like identity theft and stalking. Therefore, before you post something on social media, take a moment to think if it can be used against you.

Make it a point to spend most of your chatting or gaming time with people you know rather than strangers. And while you communicate with a stranger, do not share your personal information with them. For example, do not tell them about your location, your schedule, or details about your family. Things like your parents' schedule, i.e., what time they leave for the office and what time they return home, should not be shared. You might not find anything wrong with sharing such information during a casual conversation, but you could be unknowingly putting yourself in danger.

Moreover, never agree to meet up with someone you met for the first time online because the person you thought you knew may be different in person. For instance, let's say you become good friends with someone you met online and want to meet them. Let your parents know before going and take your friends along. Meeting an online friend alone is not safe.

When it comes to the safety of your online account, use safe passwords to protect them. A strong and secure password contains different letters, symbols, and numbers. Avoid setting passwords that are easy to guess, i.e., your birthday, the birthdays of loved ones, etc. Additionally, do not write your passwords anywhere. Neither a journal nor an online app can fully protect your passwords. Try spending some time learning your passwords by heart. Doing so might sound difficult, but using the same password for different social media accounts is ill-advised. If one of your accounts gets hacked, others will remain safe due to using different passwords. To minimize the risks, be wary of using public Wi-Fi hotspots, as these may not adequately protect your passwords (Online Safety Tips for Teens | NCDIT, n.d.).

As a responsible member of online and social media communities, report posts that are harmful to yourself or others or promote hate, discrimination, and other forms of harassment. And if you see anything that makes you uncomfortable or scared, tell a trusted adult. Don't be afraid of getting scolded by your parents if you have made a mistake that puts you in a difficult situation. Your parents are concerned and want to make sure you are okay. It is important to share such problems with your parents so that they can protect you from cybercriminals who may cause harm. So, muster up the courage and inform your parents. They will protect you and take legal action against the criminal.

Staying safe can help you enjoy your life better. Sometimes, you are the one who might accidentally craft problems for yourselves. You can avoid getting into trouble by being a little careful. Just like there is a certain etiquette for everything, using the internet has some ethics too. Everyone should follow these ethics and respect other internet users. This will create a peaceful atmosphere for all.

I hope that you now feel more confident about living alone and enjoying a rich yet safe existence online. Remember that once you post something, you may never have the chance to take it back.

In the following chapter, you will learn how to make a good first impression through your dress and behavior. It can prove to be extremely beneficial for you throughout your life. Continue reading and learn the powerful skill of making a great first impression.

9

SKILL NINE: MAKING A GREAT FIRST IMPRESSION

"You only have one first chance to make one first impression that lasts a lifetime." -

— NAS

When you meet someone for the first time, what do you notice about them? Research has shown that you can form an opinion of a stranger in the first few seconds of seeing them (Wargo, 2006). Most of the time, not just one thing grabs your attention. Instead, it's a combination of many things. However, in some situations, anything unusual in a person's appearance or behavior is noticed first. For example, if you wear a costume to a formal gathering, people will see your costume first. Here's the most exciting part about forming a first impression: you can decide what you want to communicate to others to a great extent. It is because you can choose how to dress, what facial expressions to wear, and how to carry yourself. All such things can be learned and improved over time.

Forming an excellent first impression is only possible if one takes care of personal hygiene. Moreover, good hygiene is vital to keeping disease at bay. For instance, the CDC reports that contaminated hands spread many foodborne disease outbreaks. Moreover, using an alcohol-based sanitizer in US classrooms reduced the risk of respiratory illness by 20% (Hygiene Fast Facts, 2022).

Hygiene involves more than just keeping illness at bay; it also affects your self-confidence, as does the way you dress. In this chapter, we will go through important hygiene and fashion tips to ensure you turn heads both at school and in your social life.

HYGIENE TIPS FOR TEENS

Teenagers can be careless at times. They might not find it interesting to make their bed or clean their room, but their biggest mistake is not caring for themselves and their cleanliness. Poor hygiene can cause illness and have negative impacts on your social life. It can knock down your confidence and make you suffer from low self-esteem. It can ultimately lead to many psychological issues and complexes. In other words, your hygiene can impact almost every section of your life, whether personal, professional, or social.

Why hygiene matters

Let's say Luke showers every day, keeps his hair and nails trimmed, and brushes his teeth twice a day. He is most likely to communicate confidently, make friends, build good relations with people in the community, etc. Not only will he be confident in the classroom and at different gatherings, but people will also be attracted to him due to his good hygiene and confidence.

On the other hand, if Luke neglects his hygiene, he won't feel good about himself. Consequently, he will avoid interacting with people around him, thinking they won't like him. And when he musters up the courage to make a new friend, they might not like him because of his poor hygiene. To sum up, no matter what knowledge or skills you have, if your hygiene is not in place, you will become likely to be turned down anywhere you go.

Potential problems that can arise when hygiene is lacking include:

- Body odor. This is caused when you do not shower regularly. Your body contains sweat and oil glands. Teens, especially, have very active sweat glands. Different bacteria can also get trapped if a person doesn't wash them away

(Body Odor: Causes, Changes, Underlying Diseases & Treatment, n.d.).

- Teens who are menstruating should know when to change their pads/tampons/underwear, so they feel and smell fresh. You can change your pads every 4 to 8 hours, depending on the menstrual flow (Santos-Longhurst, 2020).
- Greasy hair and/or dandruff. Your hair can get greasy because of the natural oils produced on the scalp to protect it from the outside. The production of these oils can increase with exercise, or a change in climate, etc. (What Causes Greasy Hair? n.d.)
- Dandruff, on the other hand, can be caused by dry skin (5 Causes of Dandruff (and How to Treat Them), n.d.). Shampooing properly and regularly can help you get rid of both problems.
- Cavities, tooth loss, and gum problems. Brushing and flossing can help prevent many oral health issues. You can eat and drink different things, but don't forget to clean your teeth afterward. As bacteria can feed upon the pieces of food in your mouth or between your teeth, leading to tooth decay, bad breath, etc. (Cavities/Tooth Decay - Symptoms and Causes - Mayo Clinic, 2022)

- Facial hair. Caring for facial hair is important, as it can impact your looks. If you want to grow a beard, use the right face cleansers to wash off any dust, dirt, or sweat particles. Otherwise, you can shave every few days, depending on how fast your hair grows (Saling, 2011).

To tackle these problems, you need to follow a good hygiene routine. It will help you take care of yourself on a regular basis and will impact your personality positively.

A Useful Hygiene Routine That You Can Follow

What does a good hygiene routine look like? Does it mean you spend all day bathing, brushing your teeth every time you eat, and changing your clothes repeatedly?

The frequency of bathing depends on various factors, such as the weather conditions, which can help determine how often to do it. During the summer, you might need to bathe more regularly than in winter. So, considering these factors can help you improve your hygiene routine. I have mentioned some helpful tips below to give you a general idea of a good hygiene routine.

1. Take a shower daily and apply deodorant. The shower will remove dirt particles, sweat, and bacteria from your body, and the deodorant will prevent bad odors.

2. Brush and floss after every meal. By doing so, you will clean your mouth of food particles, preventing the growth of bacteria that can cause oral health problems.

3. Wash your face with a special cleanser for oily skin if you have pimples and apply a pimple ointment as prescribed by a dermatologist.

Fun Fact: If you have oily skin, it does not mean you should not moisturize your face. In fact, if you use harsh cleansers and other products and don't protect your skin, you strip away the skin's natural protective layer and reduce its ability to retain moisture. As such, when your oil glands produce sebum, the latter sits on the surface and makes the skin appear oilier. Clean your skin using a gentle cleanser and apply a non-comedogenic moisturizer to protect your skin barrier against redness, irritation, and vulnerability to bacteria (Does Over Drying Push Oil Glands Into Overdrive, n.d.).

4. Learn to shave correctly and do not share shavers with siblings or roommates to avoid infection and irritation.

5. Care for your fingernails and toenails by cutting them in a straight line and filing your nails afterward. You can also apply cuticle oil to keep the cuticles soft.

6. After washing your hair with Shampoo, apply conditioner. If you have frizzy, dry, or brittle hair issues, consider a trim and apply a good leave-in hair mask. Use a hair dryer after showering to style your hair, trying out products like mousse and gel to make your style last longer.

7. Hydrate your skin as well as your body by applying lotion or oil after you shower, so your skin stays soft.

8. Sanitizing your hands occasionally, can keep them clean. Also, remember to wash your hands after you play with your pets. You will feel confident interacting with others once you achieve a good hygiene routine.

Now, it's time to master the skill of making a good first impression.

MAKING A GOOD FIRST IMPRESSION

Usually, your opinion of someone is formed before they even speak. So, your first impression has very little to do with your verbal communication. It is mostly about what you communicate nonverbally. The two major components of non-verbal communication are body language and dressing. Let's discuss them one by one and learn how to use them effectively to make a good first impression.

Body Language

An individual's body language is a set of conscious and unconscious movements and postures through which they communicate their attitudes and feelings. For example, when you see a close friend, your eyebrows raise in surprise, your lips curve into a smile, and you show excitement. On the other hand, if you catch sight of someone you don't like, your eyes will open a little wider, and you might express displeasure unconstitutionally through eyebrow knitting (Taylor, 2023).

As body language involves unconscious movements, it cannot be controlled entirely. However, learning about body language, the causes of different gestures, and practicing adopting specific changes in your body language can help improve many things.

The following are some basic constituents of body language:

- Facial expressions: You should work on the facial expressions you wear most of the time. Like other body language constituents, facial expressions can't be completely controlled. However, there's one thing you can do, and it can prove to be very powerful in framing your first impression. It is a big, bright smile. Research has shown that an individual's smile is usually the first thing people notice about them (Monki, 2022). Showing your teeth while you smile is a friendly and welcoming facial expression that can attract others to you and help form a good impression.

- Body movement and posture: While you walk, sit, stand, or dance, try to keep your movements steady. You should neither rush nor do things quickly unless it is needed, nor do things at a snail's pace. Choose the right pace for doing things so they synchronize perfectly with the situation you are in and complement your personality. Posture is also very important, as it can reflect your confidence (Van Edwards, 2022). Hunched posture can depict low self-esteem and a lack of confidence.

- Gestures: Your gestures can express your feelings about things around you. For example, you rub your hands together during a stressful situation. You are unconsciously trying to comfort yourself. On the other hand, showing your palms while gesturing can be considered friendly (Zumwald, n.d.).

- Eye contact: This holds great significance when communicating confidently. If you make eye contact with someone you are talking to, you can make them feel validated. It can also help build a connection and express the feeling that you understand what others are saying, are actively listening, and are interested in what they have to say (Royse, 2022).

- Handshake: A firm handshake shows confidence and interest. Whereas a weak handshake can depict a lack of confidence and interest.
- Space: The space you occupy while sitting, standing, and walking can also impact your overall body language. Also, the distance at which you stand from others can make them feel comfortable or uncomfortable around you.
- Voice: The volume of your voice and the pitch can be important in forming your impression. Some people can say things in a composed and low voice, even when angry. You should neither speak too loudly nor too quietly. It should be loud and clear enough for others to understand. The right use of voice can convey solemnity.

By consciously learning and adopting these things into your routine, you can improve your body language to look more confident. But body language cannot be enough to form an excellent first impression. How you dress can play an important role in it. So, let's learn about it (M. Smith MA, 2023b).

Making First Impressions With Your Clothing

You don't need to spend much on clothing to look intelligent and confident. As a teen, arguably the most crucial consideration you should have when it comes to fashion involves having a good balance of casual and formal clothing. That way, when invited to a party, dinner, or sleepover, you won't have to rush to the stores to shop for required items.

Staples of a Teen Wardrobe

Everyone has their own style and the right to express themselves through their clothing choices. If you are into designer fashion, you may have unique collectors' items that you can later resell or simply wear to special events. Otherwise, you may be more into seasonal, affordable fashion you can easily replace. Whether clothing is a passion or a necessity, the first step towards dressing smartly involves building a wardrobe with staples for teens.

Tips for Making the Most of Clothing

- Wear well-fitting clothes that accentuate your best features.
- When you shop seasonally, invest in colors that suit you and bring out your best features.

- Choose a style you can identify with. Express your personality through your clothing.
- Shop during Black Friday and seasonal sales to obtain clothing at good prices. Aim to buy a few quality items rather than a myriad of poor-quality clothes that won't stand the test of time (Assoune, 2022).

You have learned about personal hygiene and making a strong first impression. You are now looking clean, cool, and stylish, and you are ready to take on the world. Always keep a balance between buying the items you need and those trending in the fashion industry.

With the things we have discussed here, you've learned the nine fundamental skills you need to master as a teenager that will help you in different phases of your life.

CONCLUSION

Your teen years will undoubtedly be some of the most memorable in your life. However, they may also pose many challenges. Mastering the 9 life skills I have mentioned in this book will enable you to excel at college, manage money responsibly, keep your home tidy, and stay safe when you move away from your family home for the first time. All it takes is a curious, positive attitude when you try your hand at the different skills you discover.

Many of these skills will take time, effort, and experimentation. Some will be easier for you to learn than others. Whatever the case may be, approach each challenge with a growth mindset and celebrate all the things that failure can teach, while also rewarding yourself for your successes. Remember that you don't have to work on all skills at once; take time to concentrate on one before jumping to the next if you work better that way. You can also use a journal to record your progress and failures and to consider new strategies when things don't go as planned.

In this book, you learned that being a happy, successful adult involves mastering the same key skills that teens need. And when you learn them and make them a part of your personality, doing things will become a lot easier as an adult. For example, getting along with others and being a team player can help you make new friends as a teenager and perform well in your professional life.

You have learned how to communicate with others effectively. By becoming a good listener, you can understand what others want to say, and as a result, you will be able to handle conflicts calmly and mindfully. You have also learned how to use your time efficiently and handle different problems by keeping your eye firmly on the solution. It is especially important because you will encounter different problems in life, but if you stay calm and resilient, nothing will succeed in shattering your courage.

You have also developed the understanding that your physical and mental health are linked. There are some habits you can adopt to keep your stress and anxiety at bay, i.e., exercising, meditating, eating healthy, and getting enough sleep. I have also mentioned how you should always reach out for help when you need it because being strong and smart doesn't mean you cannot ask for help.

This book has provided you with the knowledge of factors you should consider while choosing your college and tips to prepare well for the job-seeking process. In addition to this, you have learned valuable skills like getting home chores done and becoming a savvy cook. I have also mentioned the basics of making and following a budget, saving, and investing. Finally, you learned how to make a great first impression and stay safe in your daily life and online.

The good news about life skills, even the most difficult ones, is that they can all be acquired. Nobody is born with the knowledge of all these things. Through commitment, dedication, and a positive mindset, you can be the happy, confident, secure, and successful young adult you always dreamed of being.

Finally, I would like to thank you for purchasing my book. If you think my book can significantly help other teenagers transition into adulthood, I would greatly appreciate it if you could leave a review on Amazon and recommend it. Your feedback is precious and will help other potential readers make an informative decision on this book.

Wish you all the best on this exciting journey!

REFERENCES

7 Important reasons why kids should have chores. (n.d.). https://www.
momentumlife.co.nz/stories/why-kids-should-have-chores

7 Steps to Investing as a Teenager [in 2023] - TeenVestor. (n.d.). TeenVestor.
https://www.teenvestor.com/7steps/#identify

7 Tips to Finding the Perfect College Apartment | Central Bank. (n.d.). https://
www.centralbank.net/learning-center/7-tips-to-find-the-perfect-
apartment/

10 Surprising Facts About Teens and Time Management. (n.d.). https://info.
methodlearning.com/blog/bid/98401/10-Surprising-Facts-About-Teens-
and-Time-Management

11 Facts About Cyberbullying. (n.d.). DoSomething.org. https://www.dosome
thing.org/us/facts/11-facts-about-cyber-bullying

11 Small Business Ideas for Teens in 2023 (Bonus Quiz). (2022, November 4).
Shopify. https://www.shopify.com/blog/business-ideas-for-teens

15 Safety Tips for Living Alone - Hippo. (n.d.). https://www.hippo.com/blog/
safety-tips-living-alone///

*75% of teens aren't getting recommended daily exercise: New study suggests
supportive school environment is linked to higher physical activity levels.*
(2022, June 22). ScienceDaily. https://www.sciencedaily.com/releases/
2022/06/220621141826.htm

Adams, R., CPA. (2023, March 31). *How to Invest as a Teenager [Investing for
Teens, Start. Young and the Invested.* https://youngandtheinvested.com/
how-to-invest-as-teenager/

Admin, N. (2022). *The Mediterranean Diet (for Kids).* The Nourished Child.
https://thenourishedchild.com/mediterranean-diet-for-kids/

Aebischer, C. (2023). *28 Business Ideas for Teens.* NerdWallet. https://www.
nerdwallet.com/article/small-business/business-ideas-for-teens

Ahlgrim, C. (2021, May 7). *Olivia Rodrigo says she didn't feel "attractive"
growing up because she doesn't have "European features."* Insider. https://

www.insider.com/olivia-rodrigo-insecure-beauty-standards-european-features-interview-2021-5

Anxiety in Teens is Rising: What's Going On? (n.d.). HealthyChildren.org. https://www.healthychildren.org/English/health-issues/conditions/emotional-problems/Pages/Anxiety-Disorders.aspx

Are You making a Profit. (n.d.). https://bizkids.com/wp-content/uploads/Profit.pdf

Arrowsmith, E. (2023). *How Clutter Affects the Mind's Ability to Focus.* Eaton Arrowsmith. https://eatonarrowsmith.com/blog/how-clutter-affects-the-minds-ability-to-focus

Assoune, A. (2022, September 17). *15 Easy Style Tips To Dress Well For Teenage Guys.* Panaprium. https://www.panaprium.com/blogs/i/dress-well-teen-guys

Attwell, C. (2021). *Crispy Chicken Parmesan. My Fussy Eater | Easy Family Recipes.* https://www.myfussyeater.com/crispy-chicken-parmesan/#tasty-recipes-20029

Being assertive | Childline. (n.d.). https://www.childline.org.uk/info-advice/your-feelings/feelings-emotions/being-assertive/

Best, C. (2022, November 8). *Fruity skewers with yogurt dip recipe | BBC Good Food.* https://www.bbcgoodfood.com/recipes/fruity-skewers-with-yogurt-dip

Best Part-Time Jobs for College Students. (n.d.). Monster.com. https://www.monster.com/career-advice/article/part-time-jobs-college-students

Best Time-Management Apps for Students. (2021). Top Universities. https://www.topuniversities.com/blog/best-time-management-apps-students

Bha, L. (2021, October 29). *The Benefits of Chores for Kids and Teens.* Behavioral Healthcare Associates, LLC. https://behavioralhealthcareassociates.org/2021/07/27/the-benefits-of-chores-for-kids-and-teens/

Biermeier, D. (2022, November 15). *Surprising Home Burglary Facts And Stats.* Forbes Home. https://www.forbes.com/home-improvement/home-security/home-invasion-statistics/

Biglifejournal.com. (n.d.). *15 Tips to Build Self Esteem and Confidence in Teens.* Big Life Journal. https://biglifejournal.com/blogs/blog/build-self-esteem-confidence-teens

Body Odor: Causes, Changes, Underlying Diseases & Treatment. (n.d.).

Cleveland Clinic. https://my.clevelandclinic.org/health/symptoms/17865-body-odor#:~:text=Keep%20your%20skin%20clean%20by,can%20prevent%20unpleasant%20body%20odor

Brown-Riggs, C. (2017, September 6). New Research Finds Parents Lack Confidence To Cook. HuffPost. https://www.huffpost.com/entry/new-research-finds-parent_b_11874326

Bruce, K. (2022). 15 Money Words Your Children Need to Understand. Freedom Sprout. https://freedomsprout.com/finance-terms-for-children/

Bulgaru, I. (2022). 6 Ways That Teens Can Protect Their Mental Health. Healthcare Weekly. https://healthcareweekly.com/ways-teens-can-protect-mental-health/

Cavities/tooth decay - Symptoms and causes - Mayo Clinic. (2022, March 19). Mayo Clinic. https://www.mayoclinic.org/diseases-conditions/cavities/symptoms-causes/syc-20352892#:~:text=Cavities%2C%20also%20called%20tooth%20decay,not%20cleaning%20your%20teeth%20well

Children's Resource Group. (2019, October 27). Teens' Stress is Higher Than Ever - Children.'s Resource Group - A Multi-Specialty Behavioral Health Practice. Children's Resource Group - a Multi-Specialty Behavioral Health Practice. https://www.childrensresourcegroup.com/crg-newsletter/stress-anxiety/teens-stress-higher-ever/

COE - College Student Employment. (n.d.). https://nces.ed.gov/programs/coe/indicator/ssa/college-student-employment

CollegiateParent. (2021, November 20). Housing Search Tips to Share with Your Student. CollegiateParent. https://www.collegiateparent.com/housing-residential-life/housing-search-tips-to-share-with-your-student/

CrEATive Kitchen. (2017, September 26). CrEATive Kitchen - Knife Safety Tips For Kids [Video]. YouTube. https://www.youtube.com/watch?v=lTfVOAOPUL4

Dean, J. (2022). How Many Emotions Are There? PsyBlog. https://www.spring.org.uk/2022/12/how-many-emotions-are-there.php

Depression and anxiety: Exercise eases symptoms. (2017, September 27). Mayo Clinic. https://www.mayoclinic.org/diseases-conditions/depression/in-depth/depression-and-exercise/art-20046495

DeSilver, D. (2020, May 30). The concerns and challenges of being a U.S. teen: What the data show. Pew Research Center. https://www.pewresearch.org/

fact-tank/2019/02/26/the-concerns-and-challenges-of-being-a-u-s-teen-what-the-data-show/

Does Over Drying Push Oil Glands Into Overdrive? (n.d.). https://www.vivantskincare.com/blogs/doctors-tips/does-over-drying-push-oil-glands-into-overdrive

Doulis, C. (2022). Budgeting Rule: The 50/20/30 and 60/20/20 Budget. Entourage Finance. https://entourage.com.au/budgeting-rule-the-50-20-30-and-60-20-20-budget/

Doyle, A. (2021). How to Get Your First Part-Time Job for Teens. The Balance. https://www.thebalancemoney.com/tips-for-getting-your-first-part-time-job-2058650

Edwards, R. (2022). 9 Ways to Stay Safe When You Live Alone. SafeWise. https://www.safewise.com/blog/9-safety-guidelines-for-living-alone/

Exercise Endocrine System Interaction. (n.d.). Physiopedia. https://www.physio-pedia.com/Exercise_Endocrine_System_Interaction#:~:text=Regular%20physical%20activity%20stimulates%20hormones,hormones%20in%20balance%2C%20particularly%20insulin

Faasm, M. B. P. D. (2022). Sleep Quality vs. Sleep Quantity. The Sleep Doctor. https://thesleepdoctor.com/how-sleep-works/sleep-quality/

Glw, & Glw. (2022, March 4). How Does Running Improve Bone Density? - London Bridge Orthopaedics. London Bridge Orthopaedics - Leading Orthopaedics clinic in London's Shard. https://www.londonbridgeorthopaedics.co.uk/running-and-your-bone-density/#:~:text=When%20you%20exercise%2C%20the%20muscles,is%20known%20as%20Wolfe's%20Law

Harvard Health. (2021, February 12). 4 ways to boost your self-compassion. https://www.health.harvard.edu/mental-health/4-ways-to-boost-your-self-compassion

Helhoski, A. (2022). How to Pick a Student Loan for College. NerdWallet. https://www.nerdwallet.com/article/loans/student-loans/how-to-pick-student-loans

Helping children reframe negative thoughts : Mentally Healthy Schools. (n.d.). https://mentallyhealthyschools.org.uk/resources/helping-children-reframe-negative-thoughts/

Hopsicker, K. (2022, April 25). 9 tips to help you find your first job — and nail *the interview. CNBC. https://www.cnbc.com/2022/04/25/9-tips-to-help-you-find-your-first-job-and-nail-the-interview.html*

Household Chores for Adolescents. (n.d.). HealthyChildren.org. https://www.healthychildren.org/English/family-life/family-dynamics/Pages/Household-Chores-for-Adolescents.aspx

Household chores for children and teenagers. (2023, April 5). Raising Children Network. https://raisingchildren.net.au/toddlers/family-life/routines-rituals/chores-for-children

How to help teenagers stay safe online | British Council. (n.d.). https://www.britishcouncil.org/voices-magazine/how-help-teenagers-stay-safe-online

How to save money each month. (2022, August 12). N26. https://n26.com/en-eu/blog/how-to-set-savings-goals

Hygiene Fast Facts. (2022, June 15). Centers for Disease Control and Prevention. https://www.cdc.gov/hygiene/fast-facts.html

Importance of Sleep for Teenagers. (2021, May 18). Weill Cornell Medicine - Qatar. https://qatar-weill.cornell.edu/institute-for-population-health/community/covid-19-awareness/newsletters/issue/importance-of-sleep-for-teenagers

Josel, L. (2022, January 21). Q: &#qout; What Time Management Apps Will My Teen with ADHD Actually Use?". ADDitude. https://www.additudemag.com/time-management-apps-teens-adhd-productivity-focus/

Jung, A. (2023, February 2). 12 Ways You Might Be Loading Your Dishwasher Wrong. Reader's Digest. https://www.rd.com/list/how-to-load-dishwasher/

Karimova, H., MA. (2023). The Emotion Wheel: What It Is and How to Use It [+PDF]. PositivePsychology.com. https://positivepsychology.com/emotion-wheel/

Lane, R., & Branch, T. (2023). Fixed or Variable Student Loan: Which Is Better? NerdWallet. https://www.nerdwallet.com/article/loans/student-loans/fixed-variable-student-loan#:~:text=Fixed%20student%20loan%20interest%20rates,loan%20interest%20rates%20are%20rising

Lcsw, A. M. (2022a). 10 Social Issues and Problems That Trouble Today's Teens. Verywell Family. https://www.verywellfamily.com/startling-facts-about-todays-teenagers-2608914

Lcsw, A. M. (2022b). Chores List for Older Kids and Teens. Verywell Family.

https://www.verywellfamily.com/over-50-ideas-of-chores-for-teens-2609291

Leuker, C., & Van Den Bos, W. (2016). I Want It Now! The Neuroscience of Teenage Impulsivity. Frontiers for Young Minds. https://doi.org/10.3389/frym.2016.00008

Lockert, M. (2022). How to choose a student loan to get the money you need for college or grad school. Business Insider. https://www.businessinsider.com/personal-finance/how-to-choose-a-student-loan-college-grad-school

Lowry, B. (n.d.). Culinary Terms for Kids. https://www.culinaryschools.org/cooking-school-types/kids/culinary-terms.php

Many teens are too reliant on parents for basic tasks, poll finds - UPI.com. (2019, July 22). UPI. https://www.upi.com/Health_News/2019/07/22/Few-teens-are-prepared-to-handle-adult-life-skills-poll-finds/2191563818390/

Mark, L. A. (2022, December 14). A Guide to Laundry Symbols: Find Out What Those Washing Symbols Mean. Reader's Digest. https://www.rd.com/article/laundry-symbols/

Mindbodygreen. (2022, September 15). Of All The Sleep Tips, Doctors Say These Are The Healthiest. https://www.mindbodygreen.com/articles/15-ways-to-get-high-quality-sleep

MindTools | Home. (n.d.). https://www.mindtools.com/az4wxv7/active-listening

Monki, T. (2022). What is the First Thing You Notice When Meeting Someone New? Hello Ortho. https://www.helloortho.com/what-is-the-first-thing-you-notice-when-meeting-someone-new/#:~:text=Your%20grandmother.'s%20adage%20turns%20out,was%20eyes%2C%20with%2031%25

Morin, A. (2022). Conversation Tips for Kids Who Struggle With Social Skills | Understood. Understood. https://www.understood.org/en/articles/conversation-tips-kids-social-skills

National study finds diets remain poor for most American children; disparities persist. (2020, March 24). Tufts Now. https://now.tufts.edu/2020/03/24/national-study-finds-diets-remain-poor-most-american-children-disparities-persist

Nesbit, J. (2022, September 27). Here's How Much of Your Income Should Go

Toward Student Loans Each Month. Money. https://money.com/income-monthly-budget-student-debt/#:~:text=The%20US%20Department%20of%20Education,between%20discretionary%2C%20take%2Dhome%2C

Netmums. *(2022, September 8). Blini pancakes recipe. Netmums. https://www.netmums.com/recipes/blini-pancakes/*

Nickolas, S. *(2022). What Is Discretionary Income? How to Calculate, With Example. Investopedia. https://www.investopedia.com/ask/answers/033015/what-difference-between-disposable-income-and-discretionary-income.asp*

Olive Tomato. *(2019). The Mediterranean Diet and Your Teen – A Step by Step Guide. Olive Tomato. https://www.olivetomato.com/the-mediterranean-diet-and-your-teen/*

Online Safety Tips for Teens | NCDIT. (n.d.). https://it.nc.gov/resources/cybersecurity-risk-management/cybersecurenc/tips/teens

O'Shea, A., & Taube, S. *(2023). Why Your Kid Needs a Custodial Roth IRA, and How To Set It Up. NerdWallet. https://www.nerdwallet.com/article/investing/why-your-kid-needs-a-roth-ira*

Pierce, R. *(2023, March 14). 13 Practical Time Management Skills To Teach Teens | Life Skills Advocate. Life Skills Advocate. https://lifeskillsadvocate.com/blog/13-practical-time-management-skills-to-teach-teens/*

Pinola, M. *(2016). Productivity and Ergonomics: The Best Way to Organize Your Desk. zapier.com. https://zapier.com/blog/how-to-set-up-your-desk/*

Pontz, E. *(2021). Strategies to Handle Peer Pressure. Center for Parent and Teen Communication. https://parentandteen.com/handle-peer-pressure/*

Preventing Diabetes. (n.d.). https://www.johnmuirhealth.com/health-education/conditions-treatments/diabetes-articles/preventing-diabetes.html#:~:text=The%20National%20Institutes%20of%20Health,2%20diabetes%20by%2058%20percent.balance%2C%20particularly%20insulin

Problem-solving steps: pre-teens and teenagers. (2021, November 5). Raising Children Network. https://raisingchildren.net.au/pre-teens/behaviour/encouraging-good-behaviour/problem-solving-steps

Reneau, A. *(2021). Ten Things a Teen Needs to Think About Before They Choose a College. Grown and Flown. https://grownandflown.com/how-to-choose-college/*

Resilience in pre-teens and teenagers. (2021, July 12). Raising Children

Network. https://raisingchildren.net.au/pre-teens/development/social-emotional-development/resilience-in-teens

Revolution, S. (2022). A Simple Guide for Kids' Business Plans. Small Revolution. https://www.smallrevolution.com/kid-business-plans/

Royse, M. (2022, January 6). 5 Reasons Why Eye Contact is So Critical to Career and Life Success | Better Advice. Medium. https://medium.com/better-advice/5-reasons-why-eye-contact-is-so-critical-to-career-and-life-success-eaadf294899d#:~:text=Eye%20contact%20projects%20confidence%20and,you%20will%20present%20to%20others

Saling, J. (2011, December 20). Facial Hair FAQ. WebMD. https://teens.webmd.com/facial-hair-faq#:~:text=That%20depends%20on%20how%20fast,shave%20a%20little%20more%20often

Santos-Longhurst, A. (2020, December 15). How Often Should You Change Your Pad? Healthline. https://www.healthline.com/health/menstruation/how-often-should-you-change-your-pad

Scoro, & Scoro. (2022). 17 Best Time Management Tools You Need to Check Out | Scoro. Scoro. https://www.scoro.com/blog/best-time-management-tools-reviewed/

Seconds, S. (2022). Plutchik’s Wheel of Emotions: Feelings Wheel. Six Seconds. https://www.6seconds.org/2022/03/13/plutchik-wheel-emotions/

Self-compassion for pre-teens and teenagers. (2021, June 9). Raising Children Network. https://raisingchildren.net.au/teens/mental-health-physical-health/about-mental-health/self-compassion-teenagers

Self-compassion may protect people from the harmful effects of perfectionism. (2018, February 18). ScienceDaily. https://www.sciencedaily.com/releases/2018/02/180221140936.htm

Self-esteem and self-confidence. (2019, November 25). my.UQ - University Of Queensland. https://my.uq.edu.au/information-and-services/student-support/health-and-wellbeing/self-help-resources/self-esteem-and-self-confidence

Shameer, M. (2023, April 6). 7 Useful Tips To Help Your Teens Solve Their Problems. MomJunction. https://www.momjunction.com/articles/help-your-teen-solve-her-problems_00326769/

Smith, M., MA. (2023). Nonverbal Communication and Body Language.

*HelpGuide.org. https://www.helpguide.org/articles/relationships-commu
nication/nonverbal-communication.htm*

*Spending time in nature reduces stress, research finds | Cornell Chronicle.
(2020, February 25). Cornell Chronicle. https://news.cornell.edu/stories/
2020/02/spending-time-nature-reduces-stress-research-finds*

*Spunout. (2020). 10 ways to stay safe on a night out. Spunout. https://
spunout.ie/life/socialising/safe-night-out*

*Staff, N. A. (2022, October 6). 5 Ways to Be an Active Listener for Your Teen.
Newport Academy. https://www.newportacademy.com/resources/empow
ering-teens/active-listener/*

*STREAKS. The to-do list that helps you form good habits. For iOS. (n.d.).
Streaks. https://streaksapp.com/*

*Study: Teenage brain lacks empathy. (2006, September 8). NBC News.
https://www.nbcnews.com/id/wbna14738243*

*Subiras, J. (2022, October 10). The Rise of the Sun: How Exposure to Natural
Light Improves Productivity. . Betahaus | Barcelona. https://www.beta
haus.es/post/the-rise-of-the-sun-how-exposure-to-natural-light-
improves-productivity*

*Taylor, P. (2023, March 1). Body Language Eyebrows (Reading People Is Your
Job). body Language Matters. https://bodylanguagematters.com/body-
language-eyebrows/*

*Teach your teenager to be resilient - ReachOut Parents. (n.d.). https://parents.
au.reachout.com/skills-to-build/wellbeing/things-to-try-coping-skills-
and-resilience/teach-your-teenager-to-be-resilient*

*The 10 Best Part-Time Jobs for College Students | BestColleges. (n.d.).
BestColleges.com. https://www.bestcolleges.com/blog/best-part-time-jobs-
college-students/*

*The Benefits of Plants: How Plants Can Make You Happier, Healthier, and
More Productive. (n.d.). https://effectiviology.com/how-plants-make-you-
happier-healthier-and-more-productive/*

*Time Management Statistics - 2023 | 99firms. (n.d.). https://99firms.com/
blog/time-management-statistics/#gref*

*Top 10 Factors for Choosing a College. (n.d.). Concordia College. https://www.
concordiacollege.edu/stories/details/top-10-factors-for-choosing-a-
college/*

Tuggle, K. (2016, January 11). *Teaching Gap: 83% of Teens Don't Know How to Manage Money*. Fox Business. https://www.foxbusiness.com/features/teaching-gap-83-of-teens-dont-know-how-to-manage-money

Van Edwards, V. (2022). *How to Fix Your Posture (in Just 5 Minutes or Less!)*. Science of People. https://www.scienceofpeople.com/confident-posture/

VanDuzer, T. (2021). *13 Time Management Techniques for Teens*. Student-Tutor Education Blog. https://student-tutor.com/blog/time-management-techniques-for-teens/

Vojinovic, I., & Vojinovic, I. (2023). *More Than 70 Cybercrime Statistics - A $6 Trillion Problem*. Dataprot. https://dataprot.net/statistics/cybercrime-statistics/

Wargo, E. (2006, July 1). *How Many Seconds to a First Impression?* Association for Psychological Science - APS. https://www.psychologicalscience.org/observer/how-many-seconds-to-a-first-impression

Washing Machine Cycles Explained. (n.d.). Ariel UK. https://www.ariel.co.uk/en-gb/washing-machine-101/how-to-use-a-washer/washing-machine-cycle

What causes greasy hair? (n.d.). https://www.pantene.co.uk/en-gb/hair-tips/greasy-and-oily-hair/what-causes-greasy-hair/

Whirlpool. (2018, September 21). *How to load a dishwasher*. Whirlpool. https://www.whirlpool.com/blog/kitchen/proper-way-to-load-a-dishwasher.html

Why Is Sleep Important? | NHLBI, NIH. (2022, March 24). NHLBI, NIH. https://www.nhlbi.nih.gov/health/sleep/why-sleep-important

Why Teenagers Are So Impulsive. (2023, April 24). Science | AAAS. https://www.science.org/content/article/why-teenagers-are-so-impulsive

Whyte, A. (2021, February 1). *CDC Guidelines on Exercise and Activity for Teens*. Evolve Treatment Centers. https://evolvetreatment.com/blog/teen-exercise-activity-guidelines/

Woods, J. R. (2015, June 8). *11 Financial Words All Parents Should Teach Their Kids*. Forbes. https://www.forbes.com/sites/jenniferwoods/2015/06/08/11-financial-words-all-parents-should-teach-their-kids/?sh=6556ef1372e9

Youth Physical Activity Guidelines | Physical Activity | Healthy Schools |

CDC. (n.d.). *https://www.cdc.gov/healthyschools/physicalactivity/ guidelines.htm*

Zumwald, T. (n.d.). *Do's and don'ts: Hand gestures when public speaking. www.linkedin.com. https://www.linkedin.com/pulse/dos-donts-hand-gestures-when-public-speaking-teresa-zumwald*